INDEPENDENT BLACK LEADERSHIP
IN AMERICA

•

MINISTER LOUIS FARRAKHAN
DR. LENORA FULANI
REVEREND AL SHARPTON

INDEPENDENT BLACK LEADERSHIP IN AMERICA

MINISTER LOUIS FARRAKHAN

DR. LENORA FULANI

REVEREND AL SHARPTON

Introduction by William Pleasant

Castillo

INTERNATIONAL PUBLICATIONS

Editors: Gabrielle Kurlander, Jacqueline Salit
Assistant Editors: Mary Fridley, Phyllis Goldberg, Michael Klein
Research Assistant: Rachel Massad
Production Manager: Diane Stiles
Production: Castillo Collective/Ilene Advertising —
Roy Chambers, Ilene Hinden, Ken Hughes, Jeff Williamson
Cover Art Direction and Design: Ann Decker
Cover Illustration: Michael Mitchell
Book Design: Ilene Hinden, Jeff Williamson
Chief Proofreader: Margo Grant

CONTENTS

INTRODUCTION

The African American community is no stranger to political conflict, often bordering on open warfare. As long as people of African descent have labored and suffered on the shores of this "North American wilderness," struggle among diverse political tendencies has gone on to define the path to empowerment and ultimately liberation.

In the 18th century the slave-poet Phyllis Wheatley argued for Black human rights in the name of fulfilling the ideals of white Protestantism. A little later, Denmark Vesey proposed that the quickest way to liberation was over the dead bodies of white slave owners. Frederick Douglass went to his grave insisting that the democratic principles embodied in the US Constitution — with the post-Civil War additions of the 13th, 14th and 15th Amendments — held the key to African freedom and development. Other Black leaders, like Paul Cuffe and James Turner, urged the mass repatriation of Blacks back to Africa as a solution to racial oppression in America. The Tuskegee academic Booker T. Washington led the movement for Black self-determination through the apolitical accumulation of private property, while the Berlin-trained W.E.B. DuBois agitated for direct political confrontation with the racist status quo. Cyril P. Briggs and the 3,000-strong African Blood Brotherhood saw the solution to Black degradation and colonialism in a multi-racial American recapitulation of Russia's 1917 Bolshevik revolution. Meanwhile, many Black leaders advised the Black community to accommodate itself to oppression and/or pray for the intercession of the deity.

Since 1619, when the first Africans were sold into bondage in Virginia, these political tendencies and their various hybrids have vied for ideological/political hegemony in the struggle for leadership of the African American community. That struggle continues today and it is as ferocious as ever.

The Reverend Alfred Sharpton, Dr. Lenora Fulani and Minister Louis Farrakhan are the leaders of today's Black liberation movement. To many, that sounds like a tall claim. Some might even argue that there is no Black liberation movement in the 1990s. But no one would deny that the 1980s witnessed a stark political polarization in the Black community. The old Black united front against *de jure* discrimination and segregation has dissolved into several political trends, more often than not defined by the social status of their proponents. No longer are the political demands of the Black establishment — usually agitation for greater assimilation into the great white consumerist melting pot — necessarily in sync with the demands of poor and

7

working class Black people.

The political hegemony of the Black establishment is under severe challenge. Farrakhan, Sharpton and Fulani, as leaders of the disenfranchised majority of the Black community, are the organizers of that challenge. Call it Black liberation, militancy or sheer madness, but a movement is underway which — due to a specific set of historical circumstances — is smashing the old categories of leftist politics in the US. In many respects Fulani, Sharpton and Farrakhan lead a movement that they (meaning their heretofore disorganized constituencies) made, in struggle; it is this independent history, principle and practice that stand at the crux of their ever-evolving political collision with the Establishment (left, center, right, Black, white and otherwise).

The dominant contemporary ideological/political conflict within the African American community is the fight over the relationship of Black and progressive America to the Democratic Party. Since the Franklin Roosevelt-led New Deal era, the African American population has supported the Democratic Party as the party of reform. It has religiously cast its votes for Democratic candidates on the assumption that they would translate Black demands for expanded democracy, jobs, quality education, humane health care, decent housing and human rights into social policy. And indeed, it was President Lyndon B. Johnson, a Democrat — pressured by Dr. Martin Luther King, Jr.'s non-violent Black-led and multi-racial populist movement, coupled with Black urban rebellion — who in the 60s pushed through the Voting Rights Act and Civil Rights Act which in effect removed the foundation of de jure segregation throughout the country. Under the banner of civil rights, the Democratic Party successfully organized the heretofore disenfranchised Black electorate into its pro-corporate and militaristic coalition with organized labor, Jews and liberal whites.

The long march of the Black masses into the Democratic Party did not come without strident protest. Both Malcolm X and Dr. King had warned of the dangers inherent in African Americans placing their political aspirations in the hands of the Democratic Party. They taught that the two-party political monopoly — the instrument of white corporate America — could never, by its very nature, permit self-determination for Blacks or any other oppressed strata of society. Malcolm X compared the Democrats and their Republican Party twin to the "fox and the wolf." Dr. King, in the months before his 1968 assassination, contemplated an independent Presidential candidacy with the anti-Viet Nam war activist Dr. Benjamin Spock, out of his disillusionment with the two-party system's inability

8

to effect any sort of substantive change in the American policy of war against the poor — at home and abroad. The Black Panther Party urged African Americans to dump the Democrats, and to that end joined with student radicals to form California's Peace and Freedom Party — for years America's only socialist party with permanent ballot status.

In many respects, the post-1968 Black liberation movement has been dominated by the question of how to break the Democratic Party's political stranglehold on the African American community. Every Black protest against retrograde social policy has been an objective challenge to the Democratic Party, which controls the government apparatus in every urban center where Black people reside. The Democratic Party is also the lord and master of the rural Deep South, home to 50% or more of the Black population.

At the National Black Political Convention held in Gary, Indiana in 1972, Gary's mayor at the time, Richard Hatcher, and other Black activists argued for an independent Black-led electoral party that would consolidate the political gains and social motion generated by the uprisings of the late 60s. Black political independence was placed on the agenda, but the convention decided to forego a break with the bi-partisan political monopoly in favor of electing more Blacks to public office. With Black faces in high places, so the opponents of an independent party argued, the Black Agenda could be, through a series of decrees, made the law of the land. A third party was unnecessary, their reasoning went; only a solid Black voting bloc was required.

After 1972 an urban Black electoral front succeeded in putting scores of mayors and legislators into office. Over a period of 18 years the number of Black elected officials increased by more than 365%. The Black Belt South turned in even more stupendous figures. Birmingham, Alabama — the city that had gained international notoriety as a symbol of southern reaction, elected a Black mayor named Richard Arrington. In Atlanta, Cleveland, Detroit, Chicago, Los Angeles, Philadelphia, New York City and scores of other major urban centers around the country, the mayor's mantle has fallen onto Black shoulders over the last two decades. Twenty-three Blacks sit in the US House of Representatives and hundreds more sit in state and county legislatures today. The strategy of organizing Black voting blocs to elect Blacks to office has been a sterling success. Yet the *raison d'etre* for the strategy of placing African Americans in elected office has not been vindicated. As African Americans have moved into local, state and national office, ostensibly to

9

ameliorate the plight of poor and working people, the living standard of the Black community has plunged downward. Disease, drug abuse, homelessness, underemployment and hopelessness grip Black America as never before.

Black participation in government leadership was touted as the path to Black empowerment. But as a whole, Black elected officials, even individuals sincerely dedicated to serving their communities, have failed to translate the strategy of "Black Empowerment" into the institutionalization of the Black Agenda as social policy. Cops still prowl Black and Latino neighborhoods carrying out random executions of young men and women with the sanction of the judicial system. The mayor may be Black, even the chief of police may be Black, but the racist slaughter continues unabated.

The impotence of the Black governmental strata — even those credited with the best of intentions — was prophesied in the admonitions of Malcolm, King and the Panthers. If their teaching could be summed up in a single slogan, it would go like this: Black liberation calls for nothing less than political independence! While Black people may elect candidates who are Black, their votes are ultimately cast for the Democratic Party — an anti-poor, anti-Black party of corporate America. It would not be unfair to assert that in the last two decades a stratum of the Black middle class has opportunized off the righteous anger and progressive sentiments of poor and working African Americans, to become brokers of the Black bloc vote to the Democratic Party, not for Black liberation.

Though the anti-racist and anti-machine sentiments within the Black community may have crystallized in Black electoral insurgencies, as in the case of Boston's Mel King and Chicago's Harold Washington, these rebellions took place within the structurally racist Democratic Party. Mel King lost, but Harold Washington won the mayoralty of Chicago. In the end, the results were the same — the white supremacist Democratic Party dictated social policy. Harold Washington, blasted into office by one of the most powerful poor people's movements of this century, spent his first term battling with the racist Ed Vrdolyak and the majoritarian white supremacist bloc of the Chicago city council. For four years Washington fought on behalf of the Black Agenda, the poor and working people's political platform, while Ted Kennedy, Paul Simon, Mario Cuomo, et al. — the leading lights of Democratic liberalism — wouldn't lift a finger to rein in their party's local racists. And when Washington died of a heart attack during his second term — by then he had the city council majority — the mayor's

10

office quickly returned (with the open support of Democratic National Committee chairman Ron Brown, an African American) to Richard Daley, Jr. and the regular Cook County Democratic Party machine.

Since 1972 a great deal of water — and, tragically, blood — have flowed under the bridge of Black politics. The Black empowerment strategy, based on the election of Democrats — Black and white — has played itself out to its conclusion. Jesse Jackson's 1984 and 1988 campaigns for the Democratic Party Presidential nomination were just the icing on the moldy cake.

Coupled with King's Boston loss, the betrayal of Washington by the Democratic Party liberal elite and Wilson Goode's 1985 summary execution of eleven Black men, women and children, the Jackson campaigns were the political basis of the renewed call for Black political independence.

Jackson's 1984 campaign was run on an explicitly pro-Black and pro-progressive platform. When he privately described New York City as "Hymietown" he was vilified by the press. Erstwhile Jewish liberals stepped forward to denounce Jackson's "anti-Semitism" and to silence his support for Palestinian self-determination. At the behest of the Democratic Party leadership, Jews led the anti-Jackson and consequently anti-left onslaught. When Jewish rightists — chiefly the Jewish Defense League and the Jewish Defense Organization — threatened the Black Presidential candidate with assassination, the leader of the Nation of Islam, Minister Louis Farrakhan, dispatched his Fruit of Islam security force to protect him. Farrakhan enraged the media and the power elite of both parties with his calls for Black self-defense and his denunciation of Black Democratic Party officialdom for its willingness to join the Zionist-led chorus against Jackson and himself.

Despite the open hostility of the Democratic Party leadership, Jackson's left-of-center program attracted nearly a third of the Democratic Party primary vote in 1984 but — given the unfairness of the party rules — a much smaller proportion of convention delegates. The Democratic Party's hysterical rejection of Jackson's Rainbow Coalition pushed Black-led independent electoral politics back onto the national agenda. There was open talk on the floor of the San Francisco convention that the Jackson delegates should walk out and continue Jesse's candidacy on an independent ticket. But in 1984 the electoral power of the African American and broader progressive constituencies was still hostage to Jackson's strategic allegiance to the Democratic Party. Who can forget Jackson's humiliating public apology at the 1984 Democratic Convention? He made his

11

peace with the party and threw his support behind organization man Walter Mondale in hopes of exchanging a guaranteed Black bloc vote for Mondale for party rule concessions. That never happened. As for the Black Agenda, its inclusion as a set of planks in the Democratic Party platform was ruled out of order from Jump Street.

The Democratic Party elite had rightly assessed that a Jackson insurgency could have no teeth as long as it was unwilling to break away from the party. Without the threat of an independent political challenge — in which Jackson's Rainbow constituencies rallied behind a third party candidate and thus splintered the Democratic Party's decades-old minority/labor/progressive voting bloc — the party would have no reason to grant concessions of any kind to its left wing, even if that wing consisted of one third of its voters. Ted Kennedy, Mario Cuomo, Mondale and Company knew that the Jackson insurgency literally had no option but to back the machine-appointed national ticket. The Rainbow had no clout in the Democratic Party inferno.

As the Jackson-led Rainbow collapsed back into the rightward drifting Democratic Party, the New Alliance Party's 33-state independent Presidential bid broached the viability of a national Black-led third party. Dennis Serrette, a Black trade unionist, ran on the New Alliance Party line and received over 60,000 votes. NAP surmounted a veritable wall of discriminatory election laws, anti-Reagan (which translated into pro-Democratic Party) hysteria and the open hostility of the white-dominated orthodox US left. NAP's 1984 Presidential campaign put Black-led, multi-racial independent electoral politics on the national map and carved out the contours of what would become its "Two Roads Are Better Than One" strategy in 1988.

The contours of Black politics today have been strongly determined by the experience of 1984. The forces arrayed around Jesse Jackson, the national Rainbow Coalition, Inc. — ostensibly a leftist faction of the rightist-led Democratic Party — continue to argue that Black political empowerment can be achieved through winning friends and influence within the Democratic Party. From 1984 on, Jackson and a motley crew of political mercenaries and elected officials, tailed by an assortment of social democrats, single-issue hucksters and the Communist Party USA, set about winning the 1988 Democratic nomination or at least gaining an institutional niche for themselves inside the party. Their aim was to re-constitute the old popular front New Deal coalition — Blacks, Jews, labor and white progressives — into a Jackson-led front against the regular Democratic Party machine. In a sense, the Jackson-led front strategically oriented to taking over the Democratic Party by employing a Black voting bloc augmented by liberal whites.

Backed by the Black political establishment (which for the most part had rejected his 1984 bid) and basking in the national political limelight, Jackson's strategy was to mobilize enough Black voters to participate in the primary and enough white voters who would respond to his more inclusive, if less militant, politic to take advantage of the split among white voters over Dukakis and Gore and thereby arrive at the convention with a plurality of delegates. This strategy, however, met the firm and ruthless resistance of the Democratic Party patriarchs and their ultimate front runner, Dukakis. Jesse Jackson and the Black vote were once again relegated to the "automatic" category, requiring no programmatic concessions and no place on the ticket.

Yet from the experience of 1984 a new political development had taken place. Where once the radical elements of the Black political community had been fragmented and marginal, harried by the police and mired in sectarian strife, a new coalition of forces dedicated to radical Black political independence emerged. At its core was the 50-state independent Presidential candidacy of Lenora Fulani, who had articulated her "Two Roads Are Better Than One" plan in early 1987 — to support Jackson's Presidential primary run while preparing for the eventuality that the racism of the Democratic Party would deny him the nomination. Fulani argued that by its very nature, the two-party political monopoly disenfranchised the majority of the American people. Moreover, she declared, the effective means for ensuring Black — and Latino, Native American and gay — political self-determination lay in building an independent movement and party which could break the Democrats' stranglehold on Black politics at the polls and on the streets. The Fulani candidacy, based among the poorest strata of the Black working class, drew support from Farrakhan and the United African Movement's Reverend Al Sharpton. And this new independent bloc, which had begun taking shape as early as 1985, coalesced into what would become the new left of the 1990s, the ideological/political heirs to the pro-people leadership of Malcolm, King and the Panthers. They already had a significant history of struggle to build upon.

Tragically, a series of racist atrocities would mark out the battleground for the fight between the independents and the Democrats in the late 80s. Bent on pursuing a pragmatic elec-

13

toral strategy, the Jackson forces were quick to dump their explicit pro-Black posture for fear of alienating the more racist elements of their coalition. Fulani, NAP's 1986 New York gubernatorial candidate, was roundly attacked in the media for her outspoken support of Minister Farrakhan. In the course of her campaign she, like Jackson in 1984, received hundreds of death threats, most of them spawned by the Zionist-fascist Jewish Defense League and Jewish Defense Organization. Despite this blatantly right wing attack on a leftist Black leader, Jackson and the Rainbow Coalition, Inc. failed to speak a word in her defense. The left, led by the CPUSA, either buried its head in the sand or joined the anti-Fulani lynch mob. Out of literally hundreds of Black elected officials in New York State, only one, State Senator David Paterson, went on record to protest Fulani's exclusion from the gubernatorial debates and the storm of political terrorism that had come down on her head. The Brooklyn-based Nation of Islam Minister Abdul Hajj Muhammad joined Jitu Weusi and other grassroots African American leaders in publicly defending Fulani. The 1986 New York governor's race defined the battle lines of the struggles to follow.

Little more than a month after election day, Black New York was stunned by the lynch mob-style murder of a young African American construction worker, Michael Griffith, in the Howard Beach section of Queens. Black protesters poured into the streets to protest the killing. The Reverend Al Sharpton and attorneys Alton Maddox and C. Vernon Mason emerged as the leaders of the movement demanding justice for Griffith and the hundreds of other Black youths brutalized by night riders with and without police badges. Mason, Maddox and Sharpton enjoyed the support of the Black political establishment, including David Dinkins, Assemblyman Roger Green, Congressman Major Owens, the Reverend Herbert Daughtry and the rest of the self-appointed heirs to the grassroots Rainbow movement — until they began to lock horns with New York's mealymouthed liberal Governor Mario Cuomo. Mason, Maddox and Sharpton refused to allow Cedric Sandiford, Griffith's stepfather and a survivor of the Howard Beach attack, to cooperate with the authorities until Cuomo appointed a special state prosecutor. The erstwhile liberal balked, because doing so would have been tantamount to a declaration that Queens District Attorney John Santucci — an old political crony — and the entire Queens criminal justice apparatus were too incompetent (too racist) to try a case against a white lynch mob. Cuomo, chieftain of the New York State Democratic Party, is well accustomed to striking terror in his political underlings; the Black establishment began to drift away from Sharpton and the lawyers, reluctant to cross their boss. The uncompromising steadfastness of Sharpton, Maddox and Mason, backed up by Fulani, Farrakhan and other independent leaders, forced Cuomo — conscious that a successful bid for the 1988 Democratic Party Presidential nomination hinged on winning Black votes — into a political cul-de-sac; he eventually backed down and appointed Charles Hynes as special prosecutor in the case. But Cuomo, and New York Attorney General Robert Abrams, would not forget or forgive those who had dared to embarrass them into doing the right thing.

The tactics employed by Maddox, Mason and Sharpton at Howard Beach, coupled with the fledgling movement against racism in the streets (including a new civil disobedience movement that had the potential to bring the city to a standstill), radically altered the balance of forces in the state. From the point of view of the powers-that-be in Albany, it went much too far. Not only did the movement challenge Cuomo and the Democratic Party establishment on the handling of a particular case of racial violence, more importantly, it challenged a fundamental premise of liberalism: the system can handle anything.

Cuomo and Abrams did not strike back immediately; instead they bided their time, awaiting the right opportunity. Their chance came with the case of Tawana Brawley. When it became clear to the Brawley family that there was little hope that the Dutchess County criminal justice establishment would pursue the charges of rape and kidnapping leveled by a Black teenager against white police officers, they called in Mason, Maddox and Sharpton.

This time the liberals were ready. Cuomo, feigning a fatherly concern for Tawana (at one point he called her his "daughter"), announced the appointment of a special prosecutor to get to the bottom of the case. He named Abrams, an act of pure provocation, and Abrams in turn empaneled a grand jury to investigate the case.

Many argued that the Abrams grand jury was appointed simply to continue the cover-up started by Dutchess County officials. It was that, and more. It soon became clear that the purpose of the grand jury, and the appointment of Abrams himself, was to wage open warfare against the movement catalyzed by Howard Beach.

Cuomo and Abrams played hardball. Under Abrams' direction the grand jury sprang into action, quickly turning from a body investigating charges of rape and kidnapping to (illegally)

15

investigating Brawley and her advisors. Nor did Cuomo and Abrams stop there. They used every weapon in their arsenal, including the media. The day before a second scheduled Day of Outrage, *New York Newsday* printed the first in a series of stories that depicted Sharpton as a mob-connected government snitch on his fellow radicals. The leaks of confidential information on federal probes was clearly illegal, but no one was going to challenge the establishment's furious onslaught. The coalition that had grown around the Howard Beach movement split down the middle over the charges, with many — because of sectarianism, naivete and in some cases highly dubious motives — going for Cuomo's bait.

Still the Brawley defenders battled on, marching, sparring with hostile reporters, matching the state and its hangers-on in the press blow for blow but clearly outgunned. Throughout 1988, Fulani and Farrakhan were the staunchest supporters of Brawley and her advisors, with Fulani leading hundreds of women of color through the streets of Poughkeepsie and Farrakhan lending the full support of the Nation to Tawana.

The barrage continued, including more illegal leaks to the media (including one to the *New York Times* of the grand jury's summaries) and a lynch-like atmosphere created around Brawley and her three advisors. Eight months after being empaneled, the grand jury issued its infamous report charging that Tawana had made up the whole story and had put herself in the horrid condition in which she was found; at the press conference trumpeting the grand jury's "findings" Abrams also announced that legal action was underway against Mason and Maddox via state bar grievance committee complaints he had personally filed, and that Sharpton himself was being investigated.

There can be no doubt that the vicious all-out attack launched by Cuomo and the reform Democratic Party establishment to re-assert their authority was not without success. The movement on the streets was divided, and the three main leaders of the Howard Beach victory were facing the full legal weight of the state. But Cuomo and the establishment were only able to buy some time; a year later, the independent forces would spearhead a Black revolution on the streets of New York City. Still to come in the hot summer of 1989 was the cry "Yusuf!" and "No Justice, No Peace!"

The travesty of justice perpetrated against Tawana Brawley became a rallying cry in the working class Black community across the country. Fulani, by then NAP's 1988 Presidential candidate, spoke out on Brawley's behalf from Anchorage to Atlanta. Likewise, Farrakhan embraced the young woman's cause, denouncing the structural racism of the criminal justice system. Meanwhile, Sharpton, Maddox and Mason rallied thousands into the streets of New York City. The Brawley case wouldn't go away.

The April 1988 New York State Democratic Party Presidential primary further illuminated the depth of the political chasm between the Jackson-led Rainbow pragmatists and the militant independents. The Jackson bandwagon came into New York fresh from its upset victory in the Michigan caucus. While Al Gore and Ed Koch whipped up anti-Jackson hysteria in the Jewish community, helping to convince white voters to back Dukakis, Jackson, rather than seizing upon the Brawley case and the failure of the Cuomo-controlled Democratic machine, bent over backwards to accommodate the Zionist-led Jewish community. Jesse avoided the independents — all strong supporters of Palestinian self-determination — like the plague. Likewise, he refused to take a stand on behalf of the Brawley family's anti-Cuomo demand for a special prosecutor. Though Jackson managed to eke out a primary win in New York City, Dukakis carried the rest of the state and capitalized on the anti-Jackson Jewish stampede in the city. Jackson's hopes of winning the Democratic Party nomination were dashed once and for all in New York.

In the months before the July Democratic Party national convention Fulani and Farrakhan had several extended conversations regarding the Presidential campaign; he subsequently articulated — at the Wheat Street Baptist Church in Washington, DC — the Black Agenda, which he said any Presidential candidate who sought the Black vote must support. Fulani immediately and fully endorsed it, a list of political demands that the Black community would make on any candidate seeking its votes in the November election. Zeroing in on the need for jobs, housing, health care and an end to police terror against people of color, the Black Agenda electrified millions of poor and working African Americans, marking the first clear articulation of an explicitly working class Black political program since the dawn of the modern civil rights movement.

As the Jackson-led Rainbow writhed in its death throes on the floor of the Atlanta Convention Center, 20 blocks away, in the shadow of Reverend Martin Luther King, Jr.'s tomb, Minister Farrakhan rose before a crowd of 3,000 cheering supporters at the Wheat Street Baptist Church and implored Jesse to be a "champ," not a "chump." Joining the Minister at the podium were Fulani, Sharpton, Maddox and Mason, the Brawley family and an array of other independent and progres-

17

sive Black leaders. Radical independent Black politics had come of age.

With the support of Reverend Sharpton and Minister Farrakhan, Fulani — the first woman and first African American ever to appear on the ballot in all 50 states and the District of Columbia — went on to receive 225,000 votes in the November election. A historic 2% of the African American electorate bolted the Democratic Party for Fulani and the New Alliance Party, while Michael Dukakis — despite Jesse Jackson's desperate support — went down in flames to George Bush, having received a smaller portion of the Black vote than Walter Mondale had gotten four years earlier.

Since 1988 Fulani, Farrakhan and Sharpton have grown even closer, and with them their political constituencies. Nowhere was this more evident than in the upheaval surrounding the execution of Brooklyn teenager Yusuf Hawkins. Shot to death last August after he was surrounded and beaten by a mob of 30 white youths in Bensonhurst, Hawkins' murder outraged the Black community and united it behind the candidacy of Black regular Democrat David Dinkins. A longtime machine politician, Dinkins challenged the arch-racist incumbent Ed Koch for the Democratic Party's mayoral nomination. With the specter of open race war in the streets threatening the city, Dinkins marketed himself to the white liberal establishment as a "healer" (read: capable of pacifying the Black community). Sickened by 12 years of the Koch regime, matured by a decade of Dump Koch activity shaped by Fulani and Sharpton, the African American electorate, joined by a sizeable portion of the Latino community, voted to give Dinkins the nomination.

In the November 1989 general election Dinkins faced Republican Rudolph Giuliani, a rightist former US attorney. Giuliani sold himself as the great white hope against the prospect of Black control of the city government. In classic style, Dinkins set out to break up Giuliani's white voting bloc by wooing Jewish voters, the onetime stalwarts of the old Democratic Party coalition. To this end, he launched an advertising campaign featuring his 1985 public denunciation — made at the behest of Ed Koch and Mario Cuomo — of Minister Louis Farrakhan. Likewise, Dinkins distanced himself from Jesse Jackson, also a whipping boy of the Zionist-led conservative Jewish community. So sensitive was Dinkins to the Zionists' sensibilities that he literally dumped his Arab American supporters, going so far as to refuse to be seen with them publicly. So fearful was he of being linked to the Black independents that he refused to accept 25,000 signatures Fulani had collected to

18

help him get on the ballot in the primary.

Although the African American community would not forego the opportunity to elect the city's first Black mayor, Dinkins' groveling for white votes aroused Black anger — for here was yet another political sellout in the making.

In response, Fulani took to the streets of the city in what came to be known as the "Doggin' Dinkins" campaign. Wherever Dinkins appeared in public scores of pro-independent protesters followed, demanding that he make himself accountable to the Black and Puerto Rican communities which were supporting him. After Dinkins won the primary Fulani used her independent candidacy for mayor to keep the heat on up to election day, while continuing to pull out the vote for him. Dinkins won the election by a very narrow margin, receiving only a third of the Jewish vote as opposed to over 90% of the African American vote and nearly 70% of the Puerto Rican vote. The street pressure of the independent New Alliance Party drove home the point that Dinkins would not be permitted to abandon the city's poor and working class communities of color in favor of the bankers and the brokers of real estate.

The aftermath of the Bensonhurst lynching deepened the power of the Sharpton-Fulani coalition. In a series of blunders, Brooklyn DA Charles Hynes — a white liberal elected on the basis of his role as the special prosecutor in the Howard Beach case — set the stage for a possible acquittal of the Bensonhurst murder suspects. Wary of the criminal justice system, Diane Hawkins and Moses Stewart, the parents of Yusuf Hawkins, called in Sharpton and attorneys Mason and Maddox to ensure that their son's murderers would be punished. Dinkins, always eager to placate white voters and Cuomo, effectively turned his back on the Bensonhurst case, except to join the white corporate-owned media chorus denouncing Sharpton, Mason and Maddox as fomenters of "racial disharmony." But the Black community's cry for justice for Yusuf Hawkins wouldn't be silenced.

Though about 30 youths participated in Yusuf Hawkins' murder, only six were charged by the DA. The entire Bensonhurst community united in silence; not a single credible witness could be found to testify for the prosecution. Arguing that African Americans had the civil right to walk through any section of the city free from racial attack and that the silence of the Bensonhurst residents amounted to de facto approval of the murder, Fulani and her 1988 campaign manager, Dr. Fred Newman, a Jewish radical, led a series of multi-racial demonstrations through the streets of Bensonhurst.

19

In scenes reminiscent of Mississippi 1963, thousands of white Bensonhurst residents lined the march route to spew racial epithets at the peaceful marchers. The Democratic Party establishment sat on its hands, as did the Roman Catholic church which claimed moral leadership of the primarily Italian American enclave. As the trials of Keith Mondello and Joey Fama — charged with being the gunman in the lynching — got underway, the white reaction to the demonstrations became even uglier. Dinkins and the media joined forces to pressure the Hawkins-Stewart family to distance itself from Sharpton and Fulani. Maddox was summarily suspended from the bar for his role in the Tawana Brawley case. Sharpton went to trial on 67 trumped-up counts of fraud — a jury would acquit him of each and everyone — concocted by Attorney General Robert Abrams, bent on pursuing his vendetta against the activist stemming from the Howard Beach case. Despite a wholesale assault by the state's political and legal establishment, Sharpton — joined by Fulani — continued the demonstrations, exposing the depths of institutionalized racism in New York City and the collusion of the Democratic Party in fomenting it.

Faced with the prospect of racial rebellion, Dinkins was forced to move. With the backing of Mario Cuomo and with troops supplied by the city's labor unions, he launched a campaign for racial "harmony." Along with a platoon of Black elected officials and preachers posturing as the repositories of genuine Black sentiment in the city, Dinkins lashed out at Sharpton. The media ate it up. He then bused in thousands of city workers to a "racial harmony" rally at Harlem's venerable St. John the Divine cathedral, where Cuomo, John Cardinal O'Connor and a horde of labor union hacks publicly wrung their hands over the sorry state of racial politics in the city. Their explicit message was that things had gotten out of control; the implication was that the working class community and particularly the independents were to blame. Not surprisingly, Sharpton, Fulani and the Hawkins-Stewart family were not invited to Dinkins' Democratic Party fiesta of harmony. The mayor made it clear that he had no intention of harmonizing with the restive Black masses and their leaders; he was calling in his chips in a desperate bid to assert the political hegemony of the Black middle class and the Democratic Party over the grassroots fight for racial justice in the city.

Hoping to smother the independent leaders in swathes of blue ribbons — Dinkins had urged his supporters to wear them on their lapels as a badge of reconciliation — the mayor called on the media to impose a news blackout of Sharpton and

20

Fulani. Naturally, the only places where the blue ribbons caught on as a fashion statement were in city offices. As for the news blackout, it too fizzled while the media groped about town for "responsible" leaders to parrot Dinkins' line. But the demonstrations in Bensonhurst and Sharpton's demand for justice in the murder case seized the imagination of the Black community and made Black media headlines anyway.

Under the militant cry of "NO JUSTICE, NO PEACE!" Fulani and Sharpton demanded that Dinkins and the Democratic Party follow them in forcing the Bensonhurst community to cooperate in the prosecution of the lynchers — all of them. That would be the price for ending the weekly demonstrations.

Though the first two Bensonhurst suspects were convicted — Mondello, the ringleader, of rioting, weapons possession and discrimination (he was acquitted of murder and manslaughter), and Fama of second degree murder — the independents vowed to return to the streets of Bensonhurst. A week later Dinkins relented and agreed to a meeting with Sharpton, Fulani and the Hawkins-Stewart family, along with the Bensonhurst community leadership. Dinkins and the Democratic Party had been forced to make themselves accountable to the parents of Yusuf Hawkins and the African American community by the new multi-racial movement led by Fulani's New Alliance Party and Sharpton's United African Movement.

And now, as 1990 nears its end, the NAP/UAM alliance has projected itself back into the electoral arena: Fulani ran for governor of New York, receiving more than 32,000 votes and coming in second in 10 predominantly Black assembly districts in New York City. Sharpton — together with attorney Alton Maddox, Moses Stewart and Diane Hawkins — stumped on behalf of her independent run; Farrakhan travelled to New York City to endorse her. Sharpton endorsed Fred Newman's campaign for attorney general against Abrams. And Farrakhan's Nation of Islam fielded candidates for local office in Washington, DC and Maryland.

Sharpton, Fulani and Farrakhan, the independents, have risen to the forefront of Black-led progressive politics in the US. Their willingness to confront the Democratic Party as the paramount vehicle of racial repression and political disorganization in the Black community has earned them not only the enmity of the Black political establishment and its white bosses, but also the love and respect of millions of poor and working people of color. Whether standing up to the Jewish right wing, fighting police brutality, exposing the collusion of cops and

21

judges in drug-running in poor communities or demanding that Black and Latino elected officials be accountable to the communities that elect them, these three leaders have consistently demonstrated their unwillingness to compromise the political aspirations of their people.

Al Sharpton, 36, is a child of the Brooklyn streets, a youthful companion of Dr. Martin Luther King, Jr. He can be credited with bringing King's tactic of peaceful civil disobedience through the twilight of the 1980s into the 21st century. Sharpton personifies the brilliance and brashness of the Black urban working class. Deeply committed to King's doctrine of non-violence, he is unflinching in his willingness to stand down anyone who gets in the way of his people's quest for justice and liberation.

Lenora Fulani, 40, grew up in poverty-stricken Chester, Pennsylvania. As a child, she watched her father die because no ambulance would come to her Black working class neighborhood to transport him to the hospital. She swore to use her talents and education to fight on behalf of the poor. As a developmental psychologist, Fulani battled the racist mental health orthodoxy and led the building of counseling centers practicing the radically humanistic clinical psychology known as social therapy across the nation. A Black woman in a movement dominated by men, Fulani, the chairperson of the New Alliance Party, has spent 10 years fighting for an end to the two-party political monopoly and the establishment of a viable, national pro-socialist party of poor and working people, Black and Latino people, lesbians and gay people, all people.

The Nation of Islam is America's leading Black nationalist organization and Louis Farrakhan, 57, is its leader. Painted as a monster by the corporate-owned media, denounced by the left, center and right political establishments, Farrakhan has come to symbolize the uncompromising fury of Black political resistance. Suave, eloquent, and strongly attuned to the pulse of the streets, Farrakhan has struggled to lead his organization into the mainstream of Black politics. He is the heir to Elijah Muhammad's pro-Black religious teachings and the product of Malcolm X's radical populism. No other Black leader commands larger, or more loyal, audiences than Louis Farrakhan.

This booklet is about Farrakhan, the religious Black nationalist; Fulani, the pro-socialist politician and Sharpton, the direct action street organizer. They are three very different leaders, arising from three distinct and heretofore mutually exclusive political/ideological tendencies. In their own words, they lay out their respective readings of the American political landscape and offer their prescriptions for poor and oppressed people to realize a humane and progressive future. What follows are not the theoretical musings of commentators on a distant political vista, but the observations and conclusions of political field commanders locked in the heat of battle.

History and the aspirations of the Black community and other oppressed communities have called independent pro-working class leadership to the center stage. Farrakhan, Fulani and Sharpton, the independents, are answering the call.

— William Pleasant
New York City
November, 1990

William Pleasant, an African American short story writer, journalist, playwright and political essayist, is the editor of Stono, *an international journal of culture and politics, and a member of the* National Alliance *editorial board.*

FARRA

The following is a
reprint of an
extensive interview
with Minister
Louis Farrakhan
conducted by
William Pleasant
and Michael Hardy,
senior editors of the
National Alliance, in
November of 1985.
It first appeared in
the weekly
newspaper then as a
separate pamphlet,
"The Honorable
Louis Farrakhan: A
Minister for
Progress."
The interview is
followed by the text
of the press
statement made by
Minister Farrakhan
on October 17, 1990
when he
travelled to New
York City to endorse
Dr. Fulani's
independent
gubernatorial
candidacy.

KHAN

I.

The National Alliance: *We're going to raise something that's getting a lot of press play in New York City, and that is Betty Shabazz's repudiation of you. The press in New York, and now some Black politicians and even Ed Koch, have opportunized off that so far as to say they condemn you for an alleged role in the murder of Malcolm X. Can you talk a little about what happened between you and Malcolm?*

Minister Farrakhan: Let me first say about Mrs. Shabazz that I think, after viewing the telecast in which she was interviewed by Gabe Pressman of NBC, that she did a very excellent job in trying to keep her remarks in a context and in a light where she wouldn't be attacking anyone. Mrs. Shabazz went to that show to talk about her husband. That was the reason that they invited her. But it appeared as though the show was really about Farrakhan. And so Gabe Pressman kept prodding her and prodding her, until he touched a nerve.

And what was that nerve? That nerve, of course, was the assassination of her husband. And so, she responded as a woman who has borne an extraordinary amount of pain over these last 21 years. And I — as a member of the Nation of Islam, who was a contemporary of Malcolm, who disagreed with Malcolm in his vilification of the Honorable Elijah Muhammad and forthrightly spoke against Malcolm — naturally Mrs. Shabazz could not have any warm, tender feelings for me, given the whole scenario. Proof of the fact that all that they wanted was for Mrs. Shabazz to condemn me was that when she said that I was an opportunist and that she regretted the day — the unfortunate day — she had ever met me, that became news all over the country the next day.

It is clear to me that my popularity is growing and it is also clear to me that every effort of the establishment media to rupture that popularity has been taken. Now, to take Malcolm as a hero of the Black struggle and in some way attempt to make Louis Farrakhan guilty for Malcolm's assassination is really a blow that is not just low; it strikes you at your ankles if someone is shooting for your stomach, that is as low as you can get. But the press doesn't really care; they know that there is nothing that they can charge me with that has come up in ten years. I have *never* been investigated for any part or complicity in the assassination of Malcolm X, I have never been mentioned in the early writings on Malcolm's assassination, my name *never* came up, because I was not a major player in the Nation of

26

Islam. I was a young fiery minister out of Boston — one of Malcolm's proteges. But it was not until 1971 or 1972 that I began to become popular and rebuilt the esteem of the Muslim community (which was totally destroyed after the assassination of Malcolm X) that little stickers began showing up in the subways of New York raising the question, "What does Farrakhan *know* about the murder of Malcolm X?"

Then, in 1974, this was raised again. In 1975, with the departure of the Honorable Elijah Muhammad from among us and the assumption of leadership of his son, Imam Warith D. Muhammad, my subsequent removal from New York City and transfer to Chicago, I was out of the public view. Therefore, there was no need anymore to talk about this alleged knowing or part in the assassination of Malcolm X. In 1984, when I became a national public figure again, then it started being dropped in articles, "Well, this is not the first time that Farrakhan has threatened somebody" (when I allegedly threatened [*Washington Post* reporter] Milton Coleman). Then NBC picked it up on the nightly news when they ran a thing on "death threats" that Farrakhan made to certain people, etc.

Now, what is the truth of all of this? First Louis Farrakhan (as Louis X) was converted by the Honorable Elijah Muhammad, but I came up under the tutelage of Malcolm X. He was my mentor, he was a man that I deeply loved and deeply admired, and I really adored him as my father in the movement. We were very close at that time in our development. Betty hints, and even said to me once, that Malcolm took me off drugs. This is not true. Louis Farrakhan never was on drugs for Malcolm or anybody else to take me off drugs. Anyone who *knows* my history knows that I was never involved with drugs. As a youngster, I smoked a reefer or two, or three or four. I popped a few pills but that's as far as that went. I never wanted to perform high. I never liked drinking. I smoked a little, but I never went in for drugs, so that is false.

Malcolm was endeared to me because of his tremendous strength and discipline, and I loved him because to me he was the strongest representative of the man I loved, the Honorable Elijah Muhammad. However, there would come a time when through envy and jealousy inside the movement, Malcolm began to wither in terms of faith and he began to become more angry and disillusioned. He felt that his leader and teacher, the Honorable Elijah Muhammad, was behind this jealousy and this envy and wanted to get rid of him, because Malcolm had become so popular that many writers had felt that Malcolm X was in fact the movement called the Nation of Islam.

NA: *Could you talk a little more deeply about this internal struggle and this jealousy?*

LF: Yes. As a formidable champion of the teachings of the Honorable Elijah Muhammad, there were many ministers and other workers in the Nation who wanted the attention that Malcolm got from the press, who wanted Malcolm's place of honor and esteem in the Black community, who wanted to be this warrior that Malcolm exemplified. People adored Malcolm, even though they were maybe afraid to say it. So that kind of envy caused people within the movement to start sniping at Malcolm. And it was reflected in the *Muhammad Speaks* newspaper when Malcolm would do great things, and it would never get published in our own paper but it would get published in other papers. Malcolm was a sensitive man. He began to feel this. And then, of course, he began to feel that the Honorable Elijah Muhammad was *behind* what he was feeling. And to a measure that was true, but I would offer my explanation for that in another statement that I will make down the road a piece.

In 1963, Malcolm was challenging John Kennedy all over the country, calling him John the Fox because Kennedy outfoxed the civil rights movement and took charge of it and manipulated it for his own advantage. Kennedy really was not the friend of Black people that he was reputed to be, because all the time that they had Black leaders coming into the White House — you know, the Big Six were meeting — his brother the Attorney General, Robert Kennedy, was wiretapping Martin Luther King and others. It was a very big hypocritical thing. Malcolm saw deeply into this and was *lambasting* John Kennedy all over the country.

On that day in November when John Kennedy was assassinated, the country was in shock. The Honorable Elijah Muhammad was due to come to New York to speak. He cancelled his engagement and asked all of his ministers to make no statements with respect to Kennedy and his assassination. Malcolm obeyed, to a point. Since the New York Mosque had invested so much money in bringing Mr. Muhammad to the Manhattan Center and Mr. Muhammad had declined to come, in deference to the fact that he would not speak during this particular period, Malcolm asked the Honorable Elijah Muhammad whether he could speak. The Honorable Elijah Muhammad said, "Yes you can, but remember to stay away from any reference to the assassination of John Kennedy."

A reporter came to the meeting. His name was Mike Handler,

28

I think, from the *New York Times*. And Yusef Shah, who was the captain, said, "No reporters," and turned Mike away. When Malcolm heard that Mike was there he sent the brother back to get him and Mike ended up in the meeting. Malcolm got through the lecture fine. He spoke beautifully, and then a brother got up and asked a question about Kennedy's assassination. In the question and answer period Malcolm made the now famous statement about Kennedy's death: "It was a case of the chickens coming home to roost."

PHOTO BY: D.M. FRAIRE

Minister Farrakhan at interview with National Alliance, December 1985.

As a result of that statement, the press played it up and it antagonized many whites who loved Kennedy. There were many Muslims in prisons under white Catholic guard. So the Honorable Elijah Muhammad, in my judgment wisely, silenced Malcolm for 90 days. That silence of Malcolm was as much for his protection as it was for his punishment. Because to punish him by silencing him meant that he would not be in the public eye for 90 days, which would give the public a chance to cool from the anger and hurt from seeing this charismatic President slain. It would also punish Malcolm for breaking the discipline of his leader's instruction.

During this period Malcolm, in anger, lashed out and it was then that he made known to me and to others certain aspects of the private life of the Honorable Elijah Muhammad, which had to deal with his taking wives from among his secretaries. Of course, the way it is put in the press it was a very slanderous accusation. Malcolm mentioned it to me, and of course I mentioned it to the Honorable Elijah Muhammad, which I told Malcolm I was going to do. Now, some may call that opportunistic, I don't know, but I am a loyal man to my father. The Honorable Elijah Muhammad was more than any father, and of course Malcolm was too. But if I had to choose between Malcolm and the Honorable Elijah Muhammad, my choice would

"I could have very easily lashed out at Reverend Jackson, but this would have divided our community and weakened his going into the convention."

be the Honorable Elijah Muhammad, who was Malcolm's mentor and teacher. *That's my decision!* It's painful, but I made it. And when Malcolm came out on television and on radio talking about Elijah Muhammad's domestic life and putting it in the filthy way that he made these little teenage girls pregnant, we *all* became incensed with Malcolm. I was one of many who was angry with the brother.

Then of course, as you know, he broke with the Nation, went on his own and this was when all of these "revelations" came out. Well, that incensed *all* of us. Elijah Muhammad was the fountainhead of our moral conduct. A lot of Muslims didn't believe it. They thought Malcolm was lying on Elijah Muhammad. I *knew* it to be the truth, but I also knew that the slant Malcolm gave it was designed public-wise to say that Elijah Muhammad was really an immoral man, an immoral teacher, and that Malcolm was a much more suitable man to lead Black people than was his teacher Elijah Muhammad.

NA: *Are you saying that Malcolm X designed his revelations in competition with the Honorable Elijah Muhammad's leadership?*

LF: I am saying in *anger* over being set down and in anger over feeling that his teacher did this because of jealousy and not out of teaching him a lesson because of discipline or not out of trying to protect him. He lashed out at his leader and teacher in *anger*, and the only thing he knew that would take people away from the movement was a revelation, a scandalous revelation about the personal life of Elijah Muhammad. And when he brought that out in public, many of us were very incensed about this and many of us *would* have hurt Malcolm if we could have, but the Honorable Elijah Muhammad in truth told me *and us to leave Malcolm alone!* He said, "As *long* as Allah would permit me to suffer from Malcolm's mouth I will do so. *Leave Malcolm alone!*" Those were his orders to us. And as an obedient servant of the Honorable Elijah Muhammad the only thing we *could* do was fight Malcolm in the public through words — as Malcolm threw mud on the Honorable Elijah Muhammad we defended and threw mud back on Malcolm.

In the meantime, back at the ranch in Washington, DC, this

was *made to order* for the CIA and the FBI. During that time, as you know, Malcolm's home was firebombed. And Malcolm went to the New York City police department asking them for protection. One week later Malcolm X was dead. After Malcolm's home was firebombed, there were no uniformed policemen anywhere to be found in the Audubon Ballroom. Somebody on the inside of Malcolm's own organization prevailed upon Malcolm not to search on that day. And on that day, according to Talmadge Hayer — I can't recall his Muslim name now — he came to the door to see whether there *was* searching, and when there was no searching he went back with those who were with him, got their guns, came into the audience and assassinated Malcolm X.

One man [Talmadge Hayer] was retrieved at the scene of that crime. Two men were picked up four days or so later. At that time there were 11 daily newspapers in New York and *every one* of the dailies were whipping up the idea that the Black Muslims had killed Malcolm X. Now they had to corroborate that by arresting two *innocent* men who were followers of the Honorable Elijah Muhammad *in good standing* in the Nation. I would not say that we did not in our own mind have evil in our heart towards Malcolm, but those two men were innocent. And those two men were sent to prison for 21 years. One has just gotten out, but one is still in prison for a crime that he did not commit. The government continued the story that the Black Muslims killed Malcolm so that they could ultimately charge Elijah Muhammad with the murder and use one stone to kill two birds. Since they hated Malcolm and they hated Elijah Muhammad, let them both cancel each other out, and white folks could go on with business as usual.

NA: *You said that a person in Malcolm's organization prevailed on Malcolm not to search that day. Do you know who that person was?*

LF: No sir, I don't. Now I want to say further on that these two men who were registered Muslims in the Nation have taken lie detector tests, all kinds of things on television, which have all come up showing that these men did not have anything to do with the assassination of Malcolm X. The brother there that *admitted* that he did, and in court exonerated the other two, has since that time named all of the accomplices. The government refused to reopen the case, though they have the *names* from one who is the known assassin of Malcolm, yet they *refuse* to bring that up, go back to court, and let these two men go free. Why? What does Farrakhan know about that? Nothing! When did Farrakhan's name come up? It never did! Ask *any* of them

31

who were involved in the murder of Malcolm X: Did I, Louis Farrakhan, instruct them to do such?

Who paid them? There was some money that came up in some of the investigations. You know, Farrakhan was a poor, raggedy man up in Boston with used suits, with me and my children eating beans practically every day that I lived. Where did I get money to pay somebody? I mean, this is ridiculous. But it is because I am popular today, and there's only one Black man in the Black community who has popularity dead to match my popularity living and that's Malcolm X and/or Martin Luther King! So if you can tie me to the murder of Malcolm X you can put a cloud over Louis Farrakhan and diminish him in importance to this community — and perhaps you can incite someone to murder him.

That's the plot. That's the plan. And unfortunately, Gil Noble, who like Malcolm had made a speech to members of his own profession and had gotten through his speech and then a sister came up and I mean scorned Betty Shabazz for what Betty had done on television. Gil Noble, emotionally coming to the defense of Betty, said what he said. And his fellow reporter sitting there took it back to the *Amsterdam News*, to Mr. [Wilbert] Tatum, who is married, I understand, to a Jew, and wrote one of the most vicious editorials on me, and who, it is clear, has no love for Louis Farrakhan. And it's, maybe, clear that he doesn't have any love for Gil Noble. Because the man that wrote the article could not put a headline on the *Amsterdam News*. The headline could only come by the permission of Mr. Tatum, and Mr. Tatum *allowed* that to be the headline and, of course, Nat Hentoff is coming out with it, and there may be something coming out in *Newsweek* magazine.

They really want to build this thing up — that perhaps Farrakhan did have something to do with the assassination of Malcolm X — solely because they can't bring me into any court of law and prove *nothing* like that, so the only thing they can do is try me in the court of public opinion and use the awesome power of the media to vilify me and set me up for assassination. But I say this, with due respect to the power of the media: *They can do everything that they can!* I'm issuing from your newspaper a challenge to the government of America, to the Senate or the Congress, to all of those who want to see this happen: *Do everything you can against me, don't spare me one second, and I will prove that Almighty God Allah is with me. I will win against all of you because I am right and the truth is with me!*

Minister Farrakhan at the University of the District of Columbia, March 1988.

II.

Minister Farrakhan tells the untold story of Reverend Jesse Jackson's 1984 Rainbow Presidential campaign: why he, as a religious leader, chose to involve himself in the campaign; the pressure on Jackson to dissociate himself from Farrakhan and how Jackson eventually bowed to that pressure; and his assessment of the campaign's significance — including what he considers were errors of judgment and tactics.

A key to destroying the Rainbow was, of course, breaking up the relationship between Minister Farrakhan and Reverend Jackson. In this installment, the Minister talks about his repudiation by Jackson on the advice of those close to him and Farrakhan's own decision not to respond with anger despite his belief that the move was both a political mistake and personally hurtful.

As Minister Farrakhan looks back on 1984, he examines the lessons of that intense and painful year from his vantage point as a leader of the African American people who has sought to support other strong leaders capable of leading Black people to the victories for which they have struggled so long. In our conversation with the Minister, we travel with him back down the road to 1984 to uncover the twists and turns of an historic political journey.

NA: We want to say how very pleased this paper is to be able to interview you. We've been very supportive of you and very committed to making sure that your views are put out in a way that is not distorted, because we have clearly sensed your leadership role in the

Black community, your role in leading our people to their liberation. We also want to say that we want to do this interview so that you can speak very freely and openly, because there is no other paper in this country that will present your views as you put them out. Like you, we are also committed to developing new Black leadership in this country, leadership that does not sell our people out.

LF: Thank you very much. Can I say this? It has given me great pleasure to read your publication and to welcome such a publication. I don't know how old the publication is, but I imagine it is fairly new. But when I read the articles in your paper — not just those written on myself, but the general tenor of the paper — I knew that this interview was more important than the *Washington Post* or the *New York Times*, as far as I'm concerned. Because I see brothers and sisters who cut across racial lines and class lines trying to do something constructive for all oppressed people, and that impressed me very much. With that in mind, let's get right to it.

NA: *We're going to run the clock back to 1984. Why did you enter electoral politics around the Jesse Jackson campaign?*

LF: In all honesty, in 1982 I believe it was, in a column written by William Raspberry of the *Washington Post*, he made reference to a research group out of Maryland that was advising those who invest in the cities that they should not invest in the cities because by 1983 the cities would explode, because the ghettos were a veritable social tinderbox. When I read that article, I knew that this research group was on target because the mood of our people was very, very angry, filled with despair. The rate of unemployment was going up, and Jesse Jackson came along in 1983 to decide to run.

It was not that I thought necessarily that he might win, though I felt if he could truly get a Rainbow Coalition he *could* win. And evidently others felt so too, because their main goal, it seems to me, was to destroy the possibility of a Rainbow Coalition. And so I felt that Jesse Jackson, more than any other Black leader at that time, could inspire the masses of Black people with hope. And if he had inspired us with hope, that would delay that day of despair that would cause Blacks to revolt. I felt that the police departments of this country are well prepared to slaughter our people and have the mentality to do such, and I wanted to try and avoid that at all costs. So with Reverend Jackson, I felt that I should align myself with him.

Secondly, I felt that Jesse's life was in great danger. I felt that any man that could build a true Rainbow would be a very dangerous, dangerous man in this society. And since the Secret Service was not protecting Reverend Jackson, I felt that it was our duty; we took a vote on it and all of us agreed that we not only would provide security for him, but we would raise money and ultimately we would register and vote to support Reverend Jackson.

NA: *That was actually one of the Nation of Islam's first electoral campaigns.*

LF: It was the first for us.

NA: *Why hadn't you previously been involved in electoral politics?*

LF: As students of the Honorable Elijah Muhammad, he never took an active part in the political process, at least not visibly. But there were some Black candidates that he felt very strongly about and so he encouraged us to support them. One of the candidates that he most admired among our people, of course, was Adam Clayton Powell. He hinted in his remarks on electoral politics that what we needed was strong, uncompromising Black politicians who would not sell us out, and that when we found that *kind* of person, that it was a *duty* of all of us to back that kind of candidate. I felt that in Reverend Jackson we had that kind of a man and I felt that I was not *deviating* from the principles laid down by Mr. Muhammad by supporting a Black man that I felt had the best interests not only of Black people at heart, but had the best interests of the country at heart.

NA: *We wanted to read you a quote. This is from "Tony Brown's Journal" [published in the* New York Voice, *April 1985]. This was actually after the Jackson campaign where you said, "I don't think that Jesse can look forward to my support four years from now, they felt that this was the time that I had to be dumped. He would not be able to make the great speech that he made and the little crumbs that those around him might get from the Democratic Party, they might lose that. So they ended up with a speech and they still got nothing."*
I believe you were responding to the way in which the Democratic Party treated Jesse throughout the campaign, disrespected him, disrespected Black people. Could you say a little bit more about what your thoughts were in saying that, and if in thinking about Jesse and some of your thoughts in terms of 1988, whether you see yourself continuing to be involved on a national level in particular.

LF: Well, I was disappointed, but full of understanding that

Reverend Jackson finally repudiated me on the basis of a lie. Many of his staff people, including the former president of PUSH, Tom Todd, was sitting three feet from me in this building when the statement was made and he advised Jesse's advisors that Farrakhan did not say what the press said that he said. But they really did not care. At that time I had become an albatross around Reverend Jackson's neck and they felt that this was the right moment to dump me. And so Reverend Jackson, with the aid of his advisors, repudiated me and advised those that were with him to do the same. This hurt me, but remembering the schism that was in the Nation of Islam over Malcolm X — a very painful chapter in our history — I did not want in the days of my maturity to do what I did in the days of my youth.

I could have very easily lashed out at Reverend Jackson, but this would have divided our community and weakened his going into the convention. I felt that it was better for Black people if I accepted his repudiation gracefully, asked Black people to continue to support him, to give him the maximum amount of leverage going into the convention, that he might get the best out of it for us. As it turned out, the brother went into the convention, and as you forestated, was disrespected. And it appeared to me that he opted not to fight at this convention for the needs and wants of those who stood in the rain and had suffered to bring about the candidacy to the point where it was.

I think he, under advice, opted to make a great speech with a vision of four years down the road in his heart and mind. A speech that would try to heal the wounds of this political campaign and give him a base of solid support among Blacks and non-whites, and then whites, that he could begin to build for 1988. In my judgment, it was a tactical mistake. I don't think a wise man who has the moment in his hand should let that moment slip for four years down the road (which is at best very unpredictable) because we live in a world where international policies and politics and the factors of power are changing so *rapidly*. In *one year* from the day that he gave up the struggle, hoping for four years down the road, things may radically change so that he is not effective.

The proof of what we say is the fact today that Jesse became in that campaign the single most important Black leader in the *history* of our struggle in this country. The very thing that J. Edgar Hoover had worked so hard to prevent — which was the rise of a "Black messiah" who could bring Black people together and *unite* the nationalist groups — had been accomplished in Reverend Jackson. But unfortunately Reverend Jackson was reaching for the Rainbow and lost what he had in his hand, which was 90-92 percent of *all* his people. Which would have given him the leverage and base of support probably for the next four years to concretely build the Rainbow.

But instead, by opting for four years down the road and not giving those who fought so hard for him *some* measure of victory by the way he fought — even if he bled and died to come out of it their champion, *our* champion, who lost but he fought for us — he *still* would have maintained that base of support and admiration in the Black community while he worked four years to extend that base to the Hispanic community, to the Arab community, to the Chinese community, the Mexican community and ultimately, of course, to win more and more whites. So I think he made a tactical mistake.

Thus, recognizing the fact that when the Jews attacked Reverend Jackson, and when they came out with the ads

Atlantic City, September 1988.

saying "Jews against Jesse" and no Jewish organization took out an ad saying, "Wait a minute, we're Jews and we are not with this ad," or the ad that they took out saying "Ruin Jesse Ruin," that it's one thing to win a campaign and defeat a candidate, but it's another thing to ruin a man. And it was clear that there was a vindictive spirit in certain members of the Jewish community towards Reverend Jackson.

You see, I am now locked in a struggle with the Jewish community who totally reject me, and though the Black community accepts me (I don't think Jesse could get support in the Black community without me) but at the same time he would lose segments of the white and the Jewish community if I stood by his side. So, it might be better that since this is my first step into politics that I step back out of it now and if Jesse wants to run in

1988, let him run on the steam that he can muster without my being a hindrance to him.

NA: *What if there were some other prominent Black official or someone in the community who was planning to make an independent Presidential run where there was clear national support for that kind of candidacy independent of the Democratic Party?*

LF: I would have to think about it very strongly. This was not a pleasant experience for me and I learned many, many lessons. I would hope that Jesse, if he did want to run, would not run on the Democratic ticket, but that he would take a stand on an independent party or an independent ticket free from the constraints of the Democratic Party. But I don't know whether Jesse is willing to do that just yet. But I would have to weigh that very, very carefully. I will not say that I *won't* get involved, but I can't see myself getting involved with Reverend Jackson.

NA: *Minister Farrakhan, when you were at Madison Square Garden, one of the themes of your speech was the crisis in Black leadership, how so often Black people elect Black officials out of love, out of a desire to see some change in their community, and then those Black officials turn around and join the club. That is, they become enemies of their community. How do you understand the crisis in Black leadership, and what do you see as the crux of it? Is it problematic because of the ties of Black leaders to the Democratic Party or the lack of an independent alternative?*

LF: I think it is probably some of all of that. It is problematic that we are tied to the Democratic Party. It's also problematic in that the so-called Black leadership that is moderate and responsible, is responsible to the leaders of the Democratic Party and responsible to white folks. And since they are responsible to white folks in the name of Black folks, it is very difficult for them to take very strong positions that may run counter to what the bosses feel is in the best interest of the Democratic Party and not necessarily in the interest of Black people.

So again, our Black leadership, particularly our civic organizations and our political leaders, are heavily financed by people outside of our own community. This is not their fault, this is really our *own* fault. We send our people to political office, but we don't back them beyond the vote. But it takes *money* to back politicians. Others know this lesson; we have yet, evidently, to learn it. So *wise* Jewish persons put money behind Black candidates and they invest it in Black organizations. For what purpose? Because they want justice for all? Yes, but they want justice for themselves and they want to manipulate the *direction* of Black organizations and Black leaders and they want to be in a position to check the movement of Black leaders and Black organizations if we take a position that is radically in departure from what they feel is a proper position for us.

And so, that's the crisis of Black leadership. It's that *Black leaders have become whores*, and we sell ourselves to whomever pays the bills and so we don't have too many independent Black leaders who have their hands in their own people's hands exclusively. They have one hand or finger in the Black community's hands and nine fingers and their feet under the table of some white person. And that's the way it is. So that my experience today, standing up against the manipulation of Black politicians and Black organizations by elements of the white community, particularly Jewish persons, has created a crisis in Black leadership. You see, there was no crisis so long as nobody could present some alternative to what they are offering. It only became a crisis when another voice stood up that was not controlled by those same persons that they are responsible to. The pressure is put on them to repudiate this voice. So, then there is a big crisis.

NA: *There was some study done out of the University of Michigan by the Institute for Policy Studies, a Black think tank. It was a poll of the Black electorate on the 1984 campaign that revealed overwhelmingly that Black people would have supported Jesse Jackson if he had run as an independent in 1984. The other questions in the study indicated that Black people in general supported a move towards a more independent political position in this country. I was wondering if you had seen that study and if you have any thoughts about those results.*

LF: I *believe* that. I didn't see that, but I believe that. Reverend Jackson was not ready to bolt the Democratic Party and there are a lot of implications there. He just wasn't ready to make that kind of move.

NA: *Do you think he will ever be ready?*

LF: Oh, if they keep kicking him I'm sure he'd be ready. Some mules don't move unless you hit them with a stick with a nail in it. And I think that Reverend Jackson is going to see that in the future he will have to do what he was a little reluctant to do in 1984.

III.

Minister Louis Farrakhan calls on all forces — Black, white, Muslim, Christian, nationalist, socialist, and communist — to join him in the fight against exploitation, in this, the final installment of the National Alliance's historic interview. Laying to waste the charges that his politic can be equated with that of Hitler, Jimmy Swaggart or assorted fascist and right wing demagogues, Minister Farrakhan sets out plainly a politic of inclusion rather than exclusion, of a multi-national, multi-ethnic liberation movement.

Minister Farrakhan is a religious thinker, and as such many of his positions are informed by his interpretation of the Holy Scriptures. Nowhere is this more apparent than in his discussion of homosexuality. But even as he speaks of homosexuality as a social illness — a position rejected by the editorial board of the Alliance — Farrakhan's comments are laced with a compassion and humanism which are a far cry from the shrill, anti-gay rantings of the white Christian right. Moreover, it has been his clear intent, here and elsewhere, to establish dialogue on this and other critical issues.

Likewise, the Minister's proclamation of jihad (holy war) against exploitation stands as the bedrock of his statements on Jews and anti-Semitism. Rather than betraying a primitive hatred, they illustrate a profound understanding of Black/Jewish relations in the crucible of racist, anti-Semitic, corporate-run America. For the Muslim leader, racism is a predominant component of exploitation of man by man. And as such, Minister Farrakhan recognizes a new trend in the progressive movement which has abandoned the easy reductionism of race-neutral class antagonisms characteristic of the old left and sought to round out its understanding of oppression in America.

In this concluding segment, Minister Farrakhan makes crystal clear his impact on the American political landscape. Far from introducing hatred, terror and bigotry (the mainstay of US society from its birth) into the political process, Minister Farrakhan has opened the floodgates of Black political defiance which will increasingly shake the foundations of Establishment power-mongering to its core.

NA: On a recent panel discussion about you and the Nation of Islam on Gil Noble's TV program "Like It Is," one of the things that Paul Robeson, Jr. asserted over and over again in critiquing your POWER program was the need, in his view, to have political power before you can have economic power. And he also accused you of making enemies among the wrong people; presumably he meant that you have made enemies among Jewish people.

Madison Square Garden, New York, October 1985.

LF: Well, I'm not the first to make enemies among the wrong people. The question is, are the wrong people the *oppressors* of the right people? And who *are* the wrong people? Do you mean those people in positions of power that can do me harm — are they the wrong people? Because they are persons in positions of power and have wealth, and they can push buttons to do all kinds of evil against me, does that mean that I should not speak the truth as I believe it and know it, simply because I might anger the wrong people? No, I have impressed the *right* people — the masses.

Now as far as Mr. Robeson's attacks, some of the old left are really at heart just integrationists who want to negate the fact that there *is* a racial dynamic in this country *as well* as an economic and class dynamic. I think that we have to address *all* of those dynamics. We cannot leave race out, even though race is not totally there but race is at the root of it. Then, of course, you have class and then economics all through. So the more progressive new left sees possibilities of an ally in Louis Farrakhan, in that I am not a capitalist, I don't believe in the exploitation of the wealth of the masses for the benefit of a few greedy people.

I believe that since we are living in a capitalist society we should use the *instruments* of capitalism, but the *ownership* of everything must be the common ownership by the masses of the people. I don't believe the wealth of any nation should be in the hands of the few. The wealth of the nation should be owned by the masses, and those who are in political power are only the stewards of wealth that belongs to the masses of the people. Anything other than that tramples upon the inherent right of every citizen to be not just the breather of the air that is common, and the drinker of the water that is common, and the sharer of the sunshine that is common, but they must share [also] in the mineral strength that is common to their birthright of that land. So, I think that the new left, or the progressive young left, will be more sympathetic even though they have a disdain for religion. Because they recognize that religion has been used to absolutely chain the masses, and rather than recognize any good in the religion at all, they'd rather just leave religion alone and deal with practical universal applications of principles that are bound up in the nature of us as human beings, and bound up in the order of creation.

NA: *Jack Newfield, a* Village Voice *writer, in an article titled "Farrakhan More a Menace to Blacks Than to Jews" published the day after your talk at Madison Square Garden, attacked you for not speaking out more against Reagan and the right wing. Instead, in Newfield's view, you focused on Jews. Here is one quote from the Newfield piece: "Farrakhan's singling out of Jews for attack, as distinct from whites, is one proof of his anti-Semitism, but it also shows that he has no comprehension of class. I have not heard him condemn the institutional enemies of Black equality or the real holders of power, like the CIA, which has no Jews in its top structure, or the six biggest banks (none of which is owned by Jews) or the Supreme Court, which today includes not one Jew. Or Reagan's Cabinet, which has no Jews among its members. Farrakhan frequently speaks approvingly of Reagan, and is in the habit of comparing him to Lincoln. Farrakhan's scapegoating of Jews is a detour from reality for blacks, who like all of us, need to understand the power structure as it exists." Would you comment on this charge?*

LF: Okay, let's go back over his words. First of all, Farrakhan *has* attacked the CIA. Farrakhan *has* attacked the conservative Supreme Court. Farrakhan most *assuredly* has attacked Reagan. When I say that Reagan is good for Blacks, the only reason I say that is not because he actually *is* good, but any man in a position of power as the President who puts his foot deep into the backside of Black people is pushing us more towards self-reliance. The old slave mentality that makes us think that as long as we have a friend in the White House we can negate making a friend in the Black house next door, that kind of thing works against us. When we have someone in the White House like Mr. Reagan he helps us, not because he *wants* to help us, but his *wickedness* helps us to find each other.

When we don't have a friend in the White House, we don't have a friend in the Supreme Court, we don't have many friends in the Congress, then it behooves us to cut across these religious and political and class lines to find strength in each other — then we can move forthrightly towards our liberation as a *solid* wall because we don't look towards the white father, we are looking towards each other. And I frankly think, brother, that every time we have felt that we've got a lovely friend in the White House you'll find that there's an increase in the activity against socialists, or those so-called "misfits." But when we know we don't have a friend in the White House and a friend in the Supreme Court, I want to hear what my brother from the left has to say. I'm willing to *reason* with him more because I ain't got a friend up top. So I need to make as many friends and network a lot among the masses, and in this we grow as a people. Because if you can grow to the point, as a person who is a socialist, to accept me as a Muslim, and *I* can grow as a Muslim to accept my brothers and sisters who are socialists, respecting their ideology and knowing that there is good in it for the masses of the people all over the earth, then I think we're growing through this intercourse that could only be made possible by *dear* Mr. Reagan being in the White House for four more years.

NA: *How do you understand the charges against you of anti-Semitism, Minister Farrakhan?*

LF: Let me just say this. You know, none of the Jews that condemn me as being an anti-Semite have ever offered a definitive definition of anti-Semitism. The word itself, Semitic, deals with Afro-Asian people. If I am anti-Semitic, I am against myself. You have Arabs, and they are called Semitic people. *Semi* means half. They are in-between. There is a mixture of the blood of Africa and Asia and Europe in there, and you have what you call a Semitic people. The term Semitic comes from the name *Shem*, who was one of the sons of Noah.

Now, most of those who call me anti-Semitic are not Semites themselves. These are Jews that adopted the faith of Judaism up in Europe; they're called *Ashkenazi* Jews. They have nothing to

"We are not against Jews. We are against exploitation..."

do with the Middle East — they're Europeans. So now they want to call me an anti-Semite. Why don't they call me anti-European, since they are for the most part European? They are *not* Semitic people. Their origin is not in Palestine.

The term anti-Semitism changes and shifts with the time to fit the circumstances of that hour. That has done so much to stifle criticism of what I term Jewish misbehavior. Now, Jews are no more saints than anybody else. If I can be critical of Irish people and they don't call me anti-Irish and I can be critical of Italians or Greeks or Poles or any other white ethnic who has something to do with Black suffering and I am not called anti-that, why can't I be critical of certain aspects of Jewish misbehavior, manipulation, exploitation of the Black experience? And if I do that, why paint me as an anti-Semite? Just say he's critical of certain aspects of Jewish behavior. And if my criticism is founded in truth, then don't condemn me, correct where you are wrong.

If Black people are going to be free, we have to control our own organizations, control our own artists, control the wealth that's in our own community, and whoever is exploiting our ineffectiveness in this area right now, we have to *stop* this. If this means we have to go against Jews that are exploiting us, some other whites that are exploiting us, Arabs that are exploiting us, Koreans that are exploiting us, and some *Blacks* that are exploiting us, we must do it if we are to be free as a people. We are not against Jews. We are against exploitation — that should be clear. I *cannot* tolerate Black exploitation of Black people any more than I can tolerate it from white people. So we must be clear that we are condemning exploitation, we are condemning racism, we are condemning Zionism.

NA: *Given that, what should progressive Jews (some of whom are readers of this newspaper) who generally want to follow the leadership of Black people, be doing to change the backward relations that have come to exist between Black and Jewish people?*

LF: First, we have to recognize what is truth. You know there is a Black organization called the NAACP, and it is an organization that Jews and Blacks were in from the beginning. It is an organization that has helped to advance every one of us. But if it is manipulative of the Black experience so that it is detrimental to us, then we ought to be able to speak about that. If, for instance, we are always the tenants and Jews are always the landlords; we are always the consumer, they are the producer; or we are always the talent and they're the agent, the manager and the producer — this always puts us on the weak side of the relationship. We always are in the inferior position. We don't want that anymore. If Black folk are to be free, we have to break all these kinds of inferior relationships and re-establish them along the lines of mutual benefit, equity, and justice. That's what we are saying.

NA: *At a recent meeting of the Rainbow Alliance in Boston, Minister Don Muhammad, leader of the Boston Mosque of the Nation of Islam, said very strongly that early on in building the Nation it was necessary to organize solely the Black community, but now that the Nation is rebuilding and with your growing stature as a Black leader it was time to reach out to other oppressed groupings. Do you see your leadership just in relation to Black people or to all oppressed people, and is that something that other Black leaders should be thinking about?*

LF: In the process of growth, one is first interested in oneself, one's family, one's community. Whenever we stop growing we start deteriorating. It becomes a selfish, then a vain, wicked thing. As we begin to mature and we see the linkage of suffering in oppressed peoples all over the world, we become concerned for oppression *period*, and for those that are oppressed no matter what their color is, whether it be the Irish Catholics and Protestants in Ireland who are fighting against the Crown of England or fighting in some measure to unify themselves, or whether it be whites in Europe that feel that government has not stood for the real principles that would prolong their life on the earth, whether it be poor whites in Appalachia or whether it be people in the rice paddies in Viet Nam. Once you mature, you begin to see oppression for what it is, and if you are a champion of liberation for Black people and you are successful in freeing your people to a measure, *you cannot stop* until oppression and tyranny are uprooted from the face of the earth. Anything less than that will cause you to be the very thing that you have condemned.

NA: *Right now there is a heavy set-up being run against people with AIDS, including drug addicts, gay people, and Haitian people. They are running a game on these people right now, with the ultimate aim to quarantine them or even exterminate them. What is your position on gays and on the AIDS crisis?*

LF: That is a very difficult question, because I'm not a politician. I'm a spiritual teacher. And out of that spiritual teaching comes a moral teaching that I happen to believe. I happen to believe that being homosexual is submission to circumstances rather than anything genetic or innate in the human being. I used to use a very strong term for homosexual until a homosexual told a friend of mine that they came to a lecture and they were so hurt by what I said that they probably would not ever come back to a speech that I made. But it caused me to think, there's a human being that has a problem. *I* consider it a problem. Maybe they don't consider it a problem, but AIDS is manifesting that there is a problem somewhere in this kind of social behavior.

Now, I don't know what a politician would do, but I think if AIDS is a communicable disease it has to be quarantined until we can correct it. If I were walking the streets with tuberculosis in the days when they didn't have the kind of cures for tuberculosis that they have today, it was almost mandatory that they take me off the streets. That's not a crime against my humanity; it is protection for my humanity and the humanity of others by taking me and putting me in a sanitarium until I can be relieved of that of which I am suffering. Then I can enter back into society.

NA: *Aren't you suspicious of this government all of a sudden becoming altruistically concerned with the health of the masses of poor Black people?*

LF: Of course it is suspicious, because the government has done nothing to stem the tide of alcohol, which is the number one destroyer of the people, and tobacco which is of course killing our people; the chemicals that they are putting in the foods are killing the people. So they're not really concerned with health, but this thing has created such a fear in the people, and the hysteria if you will, as it was with herpes. When herpes started to be mentioned, you could tell the ignorance of the people about herpes caused great fear. Then AIDS came on top of herpes to drive herpes into a very minor class of disease, so there's great fear about AIDS. In fact, most of the television stations, in order to secure their ratings that they might keep their advertising rates up, or to increase them, were doing stories on AIDS, so they were *fostering* the fear and were fostering the panic in the people.

Now what will this lead to politically? Mr. Koch, I have read recently, said he is going to crack down on some of the bathhouses and on the terrible sex that is going on in the bathhouses. Well, they knew this was going on all along, you see. But, if AIDS has become *such* a communicable disease now, that in Hollywood — you know I noticed this fellow that hosts the "Family Feud." He *always* kissed women on the lips. I just happened to see him yesterday; it's on the *cheek* now. So AIDS got him, it's straightening him up a little bit. And AIDS is making some who are very promiscuous adopt another extreme posture; they are becoming celibate. So *fear is* causing people to reassess all the kinds of relationships that they are having. I think in the end it will turn out to be something good. I don't know what the government has in mind with this, but it wouldn't surprise me.

NA: *At the forum that you gave at Madison Square Garden, you were surrounded by women and you talked very movingly about the role of women in the liberation struggle and within the Islamic community. How do you see your support for Black women in the liberation struggle? Why do you feel so many Black leaders seem to have trouble with the leadership of Black women?*

LF: Well, as Black men we've been castrated. We feel so threatened by the high degree of intelligence, aggressiveness, and forthrightness of our women. It only shows that we have not been afforded the opportunity under this social, economic, and political system to grow to our full potential as men. Our women have had a little more freedom to grow. There is less oppression on the women in terms of physical oppression than on the men, so our women reflect a strength that we have to catch up to. When I go on college campuses across this country, it is the women who are leading the struggle. When you go into the church, it's the women who are behind that pastor that's making things happen. When you go into Black organizations, it's the women that are causing things to happen. And so it seems to me it is a highly improper thing to *deny* the *strength* of women, the leadership capacity and ability of women, if we're going to form any society that is truly reflective of the good of the people. If it does not reflect the good of women, that society is *nothing* in my judgment. And I'm saying that I believe the Islamic world needs to reform where that is concerned.

NA: *Minister Don Muhammad once asked us to do a study on US corporate investment in Libya, and it was shown that the United States had quite an investment in Libya and does regular business in Libya. But when you got a $5 million loan from Qaddafi everyone went crazy and criticized that.*

47

LF: The government of the United States has a problem with Black folk becoming an international people. They want to keep us local so that they can keep a tight control on our activity. When Paul Robeson, Sr. found in Russia and in Europe acceptance for his brilliance and greatness, he was labelled a communist. The way he was treated on coming back to the United States was to stop Paul Robeson from infecting the Black community with the thought in mind that there were other societies that were more open and warm and receptive to Black people than the American social, political, and economic system.

So, I notice that whenever Blacks become international in their view, they become exceedingly dangerous. Malcolm went to the OAU [Organization of African Unity]. Malcolm wanted to put the problem of Black people before the United Nations. Malcolm began to become a world traveler. Malcolm left the realm of a fiery Negro protester, not in the sense of picket-sign man, but of a man standing on a street corner in the public forums of America. Now he was going into international forums raising critical issues. He had to be dealt with. As long as Martin Luther King dealt with the bus boycotts and freedom rides, he was a good Negro, bless his heart. But the moment he began to internationalize his view and saw that those suffering in the rice paddies in Viet Nam were akin to the poor who were suffering inside the United States — be they whites in Appalachia or Blacks in the South or in the urban ghettos of the North — then, you see, he was said to be communist-inspired, because that was the communist line. You see, when he began to *internationalize* the struggle, he had to be dealt with.

Now, here comes Louis Farrakhan. Louis Farrakhan *is* an international man. Louis Farrakhan intends to *connect* Black people in America with the suffering and oppressed peoples all over the world in a very meaningful way. Qaddafi not only lent us the money for our POWER program to make the products, Qaddafi *buys* most of those products from Europeans. If we can produce the products, he will buy the products from us. When the entire Islamic world sees that we produce products that are *hilal* (free from the enzymes of pork) a very healthful product that we can put on the market, then we can also have the market of the Islamic world. This would make us not only economically strong, but politically strong, in that we will be aiding the economies of other countries as they aid ours. This is dangerous for those that want to keep us under their thumb.

NA: Why do you think that the African-American Muslim commu-

48

Wall in Harlem 1985.

nity is starting to relate to you increasingly rather than relating to Warith D. Muhammad?

LF: I would not comment on why. I would just say that as I went to Mecca, invited by the secretary general of the World Muslim League, and I was accepted there, I made my *Hajj* and met with so many Muslims from around the world who, with open arms, received me as their brother in the faith. I think that experience, coupled with some change in the language of the teachings, makes my message much more palatable and acceptable to the Afro-American community of Muslims as well as to foreign Muslims who live within the context of the United States.

NA: *Why have so many Christian ministers been attracted to your message, and what sort of platforms will you develop to further the dialogue with them?*

LF: You see, the question here again is language. The language of Islam presents a natural polemic for the language of Christianity. And as long as we advanced it in the manner that we did, we were always fighting with our Christian sisters and brothers. Some would accept us; the majority would reject us because the religion [Christianity] is endeared to them. However, when we understood the language better and used the language better, understood the principles that Jesus taught and the principles that Muhammad taught and the principles that all the prophets taught, and spoke more to the *sameness* of these principles rather than to the difference of the *labels*, the Christian people began to say, "That man is speaking my language. Even though he is not a Christian he talks to me in Christian terms. I dig it."

Even among the socialists and the communists now, you find a beginning of an identification with Farrakhan — it's coming gradually — because they see in this preaching something more universal in its application that *will permit* a white person of good will to become a part of a movement for justice for all peoples of the world. So when they hear that in the language of the speaker, they identify. When they recognize that Farrakhan speaks against the wickedness of government policy that is against the best interest of America, and that Farrakhan speaks against drafting Black youth in particular and all youth in general to fight to keep the multinational corporations and the big banks and privileged whites in privileged positions to oppress and exploit the poor, no matter what their color may be, then the socialists say, "Well, good God, maybe he's coming this way, too."

Muslims believe that each human being should have *justice*, whether in God or not. If you don't happen to believe in God that's irrelevant. In this discussion we are talking about justice. We're not talking about a divine Supreme Being, we're talking about something universally needed by all of us. When we get it, we are universally satisfied. So, I'm for justice for you whether you believe in God or not. I'm for justice for the Jew, whether the Jew loves me or not. *Justice is what we want!*

MINISTER FARRAKHAN'S ENDORSEMENT OF DR. LENORA FULANI FOR GOVERNOR OF NEW YORK, OCTOBER 17, 1990

In the name of Allah the beneficent, the merciful, I bear witness to the oneness of God and to the oneness of the prophetic and human community. I greet all of you, brothers and sisters and members of the press, with the greeting words of peace — say it in the Arabic language — As Salaam Aleikum.

To Dr. Lenora Fulani and to the Reverend Al Sharpton, and to each of you present, it is a great honor and privilege for me to be here at home in New York City to share this moment with you. As you know, there has been and there is now, an unprecedented wave of crime and violence within the Black community. We, according to statistics, have learned that nearly 96% of all of the crime and violence in the Black community is perpetrated by Black people against Black people. This kind of fratricidal conflict among us is a field in which the wicked manipulate our ignorance to create genocide, but using our own hands as the destructive force.

According to what we understand, one white woman in 606 has a chance of being murdered as her way of exiting this world. And one white man in 186 has a chance to be murdered as his way of exiting this world. For the Black female it's one chance in 126 of being murdered. But for the Black male, it is one chance in 21. A human being is murdered in the United States once every 24 minutes, which means that by the end of this year, there will be approximately 24,000 murders in the United States. And 55% of those murders will be Black men and women — murdered. In the nine years of the Viet Nam war, America lost 55,000 killed. And Black people were 35% of the casualties. If Black people were 35% of 55,000, that means that approximately 19,250 Black men lost their lives in the Viet Nam war. But this year alone, Black people will die in the streets of America to the tune of nearly 12,000. So in two years, time we will have lost more of our people in the streets of America than we lost in nine years in Viet Nam. What does that say? It says that it is safer for us in an actual war zone than to try to live day by day in the inner cities of America. What does this say about government? What does this say about the care of government for the suffering of our people? It is sad to us to see that the United States government and every President from John Kennedy up to President Bush has not made the suffering of Black people of vital interest to this nation. Lyndon

51

Baines Johnson promised a war on poverty, but he also widened the war in Viet Nam by fabricating an incident in the Gulf of Tonkin. Five hundred thousand American soldiers were sent to Viet Nam and at the end of that conflict the Vietnamese gained more war material that America left behind, more gold and money that America left behind, that made the Vietnamese the fourth most well-prepared army in the world, while Black people were going steadily behind.

Unemployment is programmed in the United States so that young Black men can be all that they can never be in this society by joining the armed forces of America. According to what I have learned, nearly 65% of those in the Persian Gulf at this very moment are Black. Although those figures have not been proved true, it is true that there is a disproportionate number of young Black men and women in the Persian Gulf, ready to breathe their life blood out for the vital interests of a nation that has not made us their vital interest. We are pained at this, and we're pained at the weakness of politicians and our own leaders to speak forthrightly to the government. If Mr. Bush can spend nearly 500 billion dollars to bail out the savings and loan industry, why is it so difficult to spend a few billion in the cities of America to give Black men and women a chance since we have built the country? Our sweat and our blood have maintained America's position in the world, our brilliance has helped to keep America on top of civilization. But now when we are threatened the most, we hear nothing from city government, we hear nothing from state government, and we hear nothing from federal government. And although Mr. Bush tells us that he is our friend, if the Congress passes the civil rights legislation, which is designed to correct the posture of the Supreme Court, which intends to roll back the gains of the civil rights movement of the 60s, Mr. Bush, who is ready to send our young people to their death, says he will veto the civil rights bill of 1990.

We need strong political leadership. We need leadership that is uncompromising on the basis of principle. And therefore, I have come home today on behalf of the Nation of Islam to endorse Dr. Lenora Fulani in her bid to be the next governor of the State of New York. New York is suffering, and there is a great dissatisfaction in the city of New York as in states across this country. And whites and Blacks and Hispanics are dropping out of the political process because they are tired of the same old tired leadership, that leads for the rich and not for the middle class and the poor of this nation. In Dr. Lenora Fulani we have an alternative, a strong alternative. She's a Black woman who knows the suffering and pain of her own people. But she is

Farrakhan announcing endorsement of Fulani for governor, New York City, October 1990.

concerned not just with the suffering and pain of her own people, she is concerned with the suffering and pain of all those who are suffering and in pain. We pledge to work with and for Dr. Lenora Fulani's candidacy because we believe in her, although we may not necessarily support the New Alliance Party and all of the New Alliance Party candidates and positions and whatnot. We support Dr. Lenora Fulani because we see her as the person that is the alternative in this state to the bad governing stance of Governor Mario Cuomo. So with that I thank you, I thank Dr. Lenora Fulani for her strong stance, for her love and care for us as a people and for New York as a state, and for America as a nation.

FU

The
following
section
contains
excerpts from
Dr. Lenora B.
Fulani's
speeches and
statements
to the press
made in
the period
1988-1990,
and from her
nationally
syndicated
weekly column,
"This Way
for Black
Empowerment."

LANI

FROM ENDANGERMENT TO EMPOWERMENT: SPEAKING AS AN INDEPENDENT BLACK WOMAN

Dr. Fulani's historic 1988 Presidential campaign — which she conducted as a militant crusade for fair elections and democracy — has had a tremendous impact on the democratization of the electoral process in this country, generating a host of lobbying and litigation at both the state and federal levels to open up access to the ballot, debates, and media coverage to independent and insurgent candidates. She had the support of Minister Farrakhan and Reverend Sharpton in that campaign.

Good evening, sisters and brothers. I want to thank Latrice Rutland for inviting me to join you tonight. As a developmental psychologist practicing in Harlem, as the mother of an eleven year old Black son, and as a political activist — now an independent candidate for President of the United States — who speaks for the Black Agenda, I have a profound and lifelong commitment to the transformation of the Black man from an "endangered" species to an empowered one. I want to begin by telling you something about where I have come from, so you will know not only where I am going, but why. I was born and raised in Chester, Pennsylvania, a predominantly Black and poor city about 30 miles southwest of Philadelphia. My father, who was an alcoholic, held down two jobs. He worked for the railroad, and was a janitor in a store. When I was almost 12 he died — died the premature death to which so many of our men are condemned by disease or violence. This is how it happened. Early one morning my father woke up having convulsions. My mother and grandmother spent hours on the phone calling for an ambulance to take him to the hospital, but they couldn't get one to come into our neighborhood. Finally, a neighbor lent us his car, and they managed to fix up a home-made stretcher — my father was very tall and it was hard to move him. He died that afternoon as he was being transferred from the stretcher to a hospital bed.

I sat with my father while he was dying. I was in the sixth grade then, being taught about the Constitution of the United States and that in America there was "liberty and justice for all." It shocked and hurt me terribly to see that my father might have lived if only someone in authority — which meant someone white, someone who wore a coat and tie — had cared whether he lived or died. But no one in authority did care.

As you all know, this kind of story is not exceptional in the experience of Black people. Unfortunately, it is the rule; change the names, places and the particular circumstances and you can find my family in almost any neighborhood in the African American communities of this country. You would discover not only a history of personal tragedy largely due to racism and poverty, but also a history of the failure of traditional institutions — including psychiatry and psychology and social work — to impact on the struggles and suffering of our people.

I became a psychologist because I wanted to find alternatives to those failures. I was determined to help our people out of the pain and degradation that make us, Black women and Black men, an "endangered species." And I became a political activist because I came to recognize that in order to make our way out of our pain and degradation we couldn't, one by one, just "change our minds" about each of ourselves. We needed, I realized, to change the conditions — the profoundly unfair and degrading and DANGEROUS conditions — of all of our lives.

I want us to take a very close look for a moment at those conditions that we need so urgently to change. At the end of last month the US Census Bureau released a report which showed not only that Black people are poor, but that we are getting poorer. Keep in mind that the official definition of poverty for one person is an annual income of $5,800 OR LESS. A family of four is considered poor with an income of $11,600 OR LESS. So these figures grossly understate how many of us are actually poor, and how poor we actually are.

According to the Census report, the proportion of Black Americans living in poverty in 1987 was 33.1 percent — one Black person in every three. Forty-nine percent of Black children under six were poor in 1987. You will not be surprised to know that the Census report included a long range study "indicating" what we have long known for a fact — which is that in the past 20 years the rich have been getting richer while the poor — meaning us — are getting poorer.

Black men are dying of racism — the condition of being Black in white supremacist America. Can we save the Black man from extinction? I am not just talking about survival. I am talking about the transformation from endangerment to empowerment.

I believe that the answer is yes — I have dedicated my life to making that transformation happen — and that the key to it happening is independence. The Black man must declare his independence from an economic and political and cultural and psychological and sexual system that assigns him to a series of roles all of which are disempowering, disfiguring, dismissive and dangerous. What are some of those roles?

There is the poor Black man, a downtrodden victim, humiliatingly dependent on the small change thrown his way by his boss, by a grudging welfare system or a resentful woman.

There's the crook and the con artist, always trying to get over, always "up to something," always in trouble with someone — his "partners," his "competition," and his "customers," not to mention the cops.

There's the ladies' man, who parades his sexuality like it's the only thing he's got that's worth anything.

There's the alcoholic, the addict, the gambler — all desperately, suicidally dependent on getting high off something that can make them get away for a moment from the profoundly dehumanizing experience of being endangered.

And there is the Black man who has "made it" — allowed to be somebody in the white man's world on the condition that he forgets his Blackness, on the condition that he ignores the Blackness of his Black sisters and brothers, on the condition that he agrees to keep silent about what it is really like to be Black in America. Because as our great teacher W.E.B. DuBois reminded us, racism doesn't mean that some act of terror or brutality has to be committed against us every day. . . racism simply means that such an act "*can* always occur" any day — it means never being out of danger. For when the Black man is allowed to make it into that privileged white world, he is forced to function within a system that is fundamentally racist — a system that depends upon his degradation and his endangerment.

There are other roles, too, all equally unacceptable, all functioning to keep the Black man in his place — in debt, in jail, in bed or in the gutter, or away in a privileged world of his own cut off from other Black people — anyplace but in power.

This is as true of the Black man's political role as it is of his economic and cultural roles.

If we're going to talk about "a permanent solution" to the endangered condition of the Black man in America, if we're going to talk about accomplishing the transformation from endangerment to empowerment, then we have to talk about politics. And to me that means independent politics — an assertion of our pro-Blackness against the die-hard anti-Blackness of this white supremacist social system. You see, what Minister Farrakhan calls "a permanent solution" requires nothing less than the fundamental restructuring, the reorganization, of American society.

What independence means to me isn't a small political tactic — it's not about the election this year, or even about building

Dr. Fulani leads New Alliance Party contingent from Harlem at 1988 peace rally in New York City.

an independent, Black-led party over the years and decades to come, which I am committed to doing. Independence is how we as Black men and Black women can step out of those profoundly anti-Black roles in which we have been cast and into power.

DRUGS VERSUS EMPOWERMENT

We understand that drugs are killing our children — killing their bodies, killing their minds, killing their souls. Who is responsible for the killing? The white corporate-controlled media, all too often aided and abetted by the Black establishment — our professional politicians, our professors, our "entrepreneurs" and our "experts" — want us to think that it is our fault. We are told that we don't teach our children the right values, so they end up with a bad attitude, bad friends, and bad morals. But I don't believe we, or our children, are to blame.

Our children are dying of drugs, of poverty, and of despair because there is no room for them in white America and the Powers That Be would rather see them dead — physically, emotionally, and mentally — than alive, angry and empowered. There are really *two* drug problems in the Black community — the problem of illegal drugs that make people "high," and the problem of the legal kind of drugs, pushed by the doctors and the social workers, that are supposed to cool folks out.

What I am saying is that drugs have an economic function — they make big money for big time dealers, legal and illegal,

59

and they put a few dollars in the pockets of people in the community who don't have and can't get "respectable" work because there isn't any to be had. It's these small timers who usually get scapegoated when the politicians decide to make a show of dealing with the drug problem. The real wheelers and dealers stay behind the scenes and rarely get touched.

But drugs, legal and illegal, have a very important political function as well. Not only do they make huge profits for those who deal them, both are designed to keep our children — especially our young men — out of it: out of the world, out of their minds, and out of control. Because if you are "high" on crack or down on thorazine, or chained to a methadone clinic every day of your life, you're not in any place to fight back against the racism and poverty that brought you there in the first place.

Now you know that there are those who say that politics and psychology don't, or shouldn't, mix. I disagree. There is no such thing, sisters and brothers, as a "neutral" psychology. A psychological theory and practice that views middle class white men as the emotional, intellectual and developmental "norm" — which traditional psychology does — is not neutral. A psychology which prescribes a socialization process for children that teaches them the values, aspirations and emotions appropriate for adapting to a world in which middle class white men are normal — is not neutral. A psychology which measures mental health, "maturity" and development in terms of the degree to which people adapt to such a world and defines mental illness in terms of "maladjustment" — such a psychology is not neutral. Such a psychology is embedded in politics and politics is embedded in it. Regardless of who practices such a psychology, it is fundamentally conservative — which means that it is fundamentally racist, classist and sexist — because it validates, rather than challenges, the status quo. It is a psychology of *disempowerment* which functions, whether intentionally or not does not matter, to keep our people in our socially prescribed places, at the bottom.

UNDERSTANDING RACISM

We live in a world of differences. Most fundamental of all are the economic differences — the class differences — that divide the world into haves and have-nots. I believe very strongly that it is those class differences — not human nature, psychology, or just evil-mindedness — that create racism. And I believe just as strongly that it is only the eradication of class differences which will do away with racism.

Dr. Lenora Fulani and Vernon Bellecourt of the American Indian Movement at protest opposite Democratic National Convention, Atlanta, 1988.

Now I am not saying that racism doesn't have a life of its own; it does, just the way a child — even a very young one — develops its own ways, habits, and style. Racism in America has a very particular, and ugly, look to it. But where it comes from, its roots, are in the economic exploitation of one class by another and the need of that exploiting class to rationalize its economic activity by making it come to seem natural and necessary.

The wealth of America — the greatest wealth the world has ever known — was produced in the first place from the expropriation of Indian land and the enslavement of African labor. I am talking about centuries of robbery, kidnapping, rape, murder and genocide perpetrated by a class of people committed to making a profit by any means — the most ruthless class in history. It wasn't glamorous, it wasn't heroic; it was vicious, filthy and brutal. The development of America took place over the dead bodies of our people. And we are still dying — of hunger, police brutality, drug addiction and despair — to make them prosper.

To justify the economic activities of slavery and plunder, an ideology was invented that reduced people of color — Africans and Indians — to something less than human: savages with no culture, no society, no intelligence, and no feelings. This is where the stereotypes of racist ideology first began — the "wild" Indian, the "lazy" Negro, could be treated like animals because we weren't fully human. Our only value was in the use we had for "civilization" — meaning the class of Southern slaveowners and Northern "captains of industry," the robber barons, most of whom made their early fortunes from the buying and selling of Black people.

Yet although American capitalism has been dependent from the beginning on our labor, we as Black people have never been allowed to become fully integrated into this country's economic, political and cultural life. While Native Americans were physically removed from the scene by genocide or the system of homegrown apartheid known as reservations, African Americans have been *kept* to do work — the hardest work at the lowest wages — but kept out of the social institutions (from public schools to the major political parties) that would give us access to the economic and political opportunities which even the most exploited and oppressed white workers were — eventually — permitted to have.

This is what I mean when I say that racism can't be understood merely as "prejudice" — a set of ideas, attitudes and feelings that white folks have towards us which can be explained in terms of physical or cultural differences. Prejudice is part of racism, but it is not the whole story. Racism is deeper, much deeper, than that; it is the real Plymouth Rock on which American society was founded and rests to this very day — the economic exploitation of Black labor, accompanied by the political suppression of Black power, and the physical repression of Black protest, all justified by middle class so-called intellectuals (Black as well as white) who write newspaper articles, monographs, and whole books blaming us, our families, our values and our morals — or lack of them — for poverty, abuse, and racism itself.

But we are not the ones to blame. Keeping us and other poor people poor is what keeps the rich in business. Keeping us quiet — with drugs, and guns, if necessary — is how they manage to get away with it. And the myth of our racial inferiority is what they use for an excuse. That's why we can't come up with a "cure" for racism unless we deal with the economic exploitation that it covers up.

NEW ALLIANCES Many in the lesbian and gay community have been actively supporting my independent campaign for President of the United States. They have my deepest love and respect. In the spirit of unity they have asked me to explain how it is possible for me to support at the same time both Louis Farrakhan, the controversial Black Muslim minister, and gay rights. I think this is a very important question, and I welcome it. Now, when the Presidential race has

Gay Pride Parade, June 1990, New York City.

narrowed down to three national candidates, George Bush, Michael Dukakis — two anti-gay, anti-Black political *establishment insiders* — and me, a proudly pro-gay, independent Black *outsider*, is a particularly good time to address it.

Let us be candid. The political system in America is run by "insiders" — people who look, think, speak and act in ways that are acceptable to the very wealthy, very straight white male-dominated elite which owns and controls this country. Among the other "services" that they perform, these insiders arrogate to themselves the authority to identify and designate the legitimate, *acceptable* representatives and spokespersons of the various oppressed groupings (what they call "special interests") which in fact comprise the vast majority of Americans: people of color, lesbians and gays, women and Jews.

What is the criterion which the "insiders" use to determine who the "legitimate" leaders are? It is the willingness of these "official" spokespersons to persuade their people to assimilate — which means to give up their struggle for recognition, self-respect and, most importantly, political power in exchange for a pseudo-respectability and crumbs from a shrinking pie.

But despite the fact that every oppressed community has its preachers and politicians of assimilation, vast numbers of our people have been unwilling to go along. Likewise a growing number of independent leaders have been unwilling to pay the

63

"I identify very strongly with the outsiders."

price necessary to buy into an America that despises us. There are many proud voices in the Native American community, the radical lesbian feminist movement, and in the Black community who have taken an independent stand. These leaders are either ignored by the Powers That Be or are made the objects of all-out campaigns to belittle and destroy their credibility. In fact, it is often the "legitimate" mouthpieces for the establishment who do the attacking. Minister Louis Farrakhan has been the target of such slander campaigns. I have been also. So have dozens of other leaders of this country's oppressed communities, including the lesbian and gay community. We who have remained true to our peoples and our principles and, in so doing, *outside* white supremacist, homophobic corporate America have often been vilified.

I identify very strongly with the outsiders. I am a leader who has *chosen* to be *outside* corporate America and *inside* the real mainstream — with my people and other *outsiders*. Being outside makes it possible to serve as a genuine representative of a community or a people. Assimilationist leaders, however, typically have sacrificed this connection in order to be on the inside — representing the two parties of corporate America. Those of us who have turned our backs on these good jobs representing the establishment may disagree with one another but we all have a principled and radical connection to our people that must be respected. It is what makes the possibility of a coalition of such people anathema to the Powers That Be.

As my relationship to the lesbian and gay community has grown closer, as I've been welcomed as a sister, questions about my relationship with Minister Farrakhan, as I said earlier, have proliferated. Many of these questions reflect the misperceptions and prejudices that are purposefully disseminated by the mass media to discredit a leader who despite their efforts is nevertheless followed by millions of African Americans, including many who are not members of the Nation of Islam and indeed are not Muslims.

I *know* Louis Farrakhan. I have spent hours talking with him. He is a Muslim theologian. I am not. We disagree on a number of important issues, including the gay question. But I have been impressed, and very moved, by his openness and his willingness to hear all people. As a true leader he is always willing to learn, and to teach what he has learned to those who follow him. He is a man of tremendous compassion, love and caring.

He may make statements with which we do not agree. But he

is such a caring and uncompromising radical, with a deep and unshakable connection to the rage and aspirations of Black Americans — who have been spat upon by straight white America — that I believe with all my heart he merits the trust of all oppressed people. He is a friend with whom we may have differences; he is not the enemy.

What is most significant about my passionate support for both lesbian and gay rights and for Minister Farrakhan is that through my independent Presidential campaign we are bringing together two powerful separatist movements — separatist in the best sense of the word in that they are unwilling to assimilate into the victimized morass of homogenized, racist, sexist and homophobic corporate America. Each movement derives great strength from the pride it takes in who it is, in its insistence on maintaining its cultural and social sovereignty, and in its refusal to assimilate.

BLACK EMPOWERMENT: THE STRUGGLE CONTINUES

Good evening, sisters and brothers. As Salaam Aleikum. I want to thank Jocelyn Allen for inviting me to join you all here tonight. I am very glad to have this opportunity to speak with you about the struggle for Black empowerment. It does indeed continue.

As a psychologist I have always especially appreciated these words that Dr. Martin Luther King, Jr. wrote about maladjustment. He said, "Today psychologists have a favorite word, and that word is maladjusted. I tell you today that there are some things in our social system to which I am proud to be maladjusted. I shall never be adjusted to lynch mobs, segregation, economic inequalities, the madness of militarism, and self-defeating physical violence. The salvation of the world lies in the maladjusted."

I'm proud to be someone who has never "grown up" in the sense that, like Dr. King, I have refused to adjust to the way things are. The issue for me has been figuring out how to bridge the gap between my ideals and how things are now by building something that has the capacity to realize those ideals — to change reality. As an independent candidate for President of the United States, I received my highest vote counts from Black college students — so I know that many of you will understand what I am talking about when I say that Black-led independent politics is the wave of the future!

Not everyone agrees, of course. Since 1984, when Reverend

65

"As an independent candidate for the Presidency, I urged Black voters to teach the white supremacist Democratic Party leaders a lesson..."

Jesse Jackson made his historic first bid for the Democratic Party Presidential nomination, he has put forth the perspective that the political role of the African American community is to serve as the "conscience" of the party. That is a view which many Black leaders share. I do not.

Let me tell you why. I began my independent Presidential campaign two years ago with the slogan "Two Roads Are Better Than One." It meant supporting Reverend Jackson in the Democratic Party primaries while at the same time preparing my independent candidacy in the very likely event that he would be denied the party's nomination. As it turned out, of course, Jesse Jackson was not only denied the nomination but was openly and publicly insulted by the party's Presidential nominee.

Seven and a half million people voted in the primaries for the anti-corporate, inclusive social vision articulated by Reverend Jackson. But at the party's Atlanta convention in July, he was passed over for the Vice Presidential nomination in favor of an anti-poor, pro-contra Texas land baron whose only claim to a place on the ticket was his appeal to the southern white male vote. Michael Dukakis and Lloyd Bentsen spent the months up until the election trying to prove to the good ol' boys that they didn't even know Jesse Jackson's name — in fact, word leaked out that Dukakis had ordered Jesse to stay out of certain states for the duration of the campaign for fear that he would alienate the racist vote.

Just over one week ago Ron Brown, a Black man, was elected chairman of the Democratic National Committee. The Democratic Party establishment and their friends in the corporate-controlled media are bursting with self-congratulatory pride, hailing Brown's election as a sign that racism is dead and buried as far as the Democrats are concerned. But it means no such thing. In fact, Brown's promotion signifies exactly the opposite.

Ron Brown got the job just because he's *not* Jesse Jackson! You see, in 1988 the 7 1/2 million people who voted for Reverend Jackson were not voting for Jesse Jackson the Democrat, but for Jesse Jackson the architect of the Rainbow social vision. But the Democratic Party establishment was determined to shut that vision out. That was why, as an independent candidate for the Presidency, I urged Black voters to teach the white supremacist Democratic Party leaders a lesson — by showing them that we would not continue to give our votes to a party that rejects our Agenda, insults our leaders and ignores our community.

And — despite the efforts of the Black Democratic Party establishment to get the African American electorate to vote for Dukakis/Bentsen — Black voters staged what I believe was the beginning of a mass movement to "Dump the Democrats."

On election day Black voters rebelled against the Democratic Party and its establishment Black leadership. For the first time in over half a century Black voters made a discernible move away from the party to which we have loyally given our support year in and year out since 1936. One million Black people who voted for Walter Mondale in 1984 chose not to show up at the polls at all on election day, 1988. Two hundred thousand more were so offended by the Democrats' rejection of the Black Agenda and the calculated insults directed at Reverend Jesse Jackson that they gave their votes to George Bush.

But the most intense expression of the Black voter rebellion was the 2% of the national Black vote that went to me — in some key Black districts I received as much as 7 1/2% of the vote.

And the Democratic Party leadership were scared silly! Their response to the pressure from the Black-led left wing of the Rainbow was to choose a conservative Black leader like Ron Brown to act as a front man for a party which has demonstrated that it has neither the commitment nor the courage to stand up to the far right, or to function as a genuine opposition to the right wing-controlled Republican Party. In fact, when Brown was asked by reporters at the National Press Club in Washington, DC recently whether Jackson was qualified to be President, Brown refused to respond! No, sisters and brothers, contrary to what some of our Black elected officials would like us to think, Ron Brown is no "concession" to the Rainbow or to the Black Agenda. He is the Democrats' *alternative* to that inclusive social vision and to that progressive agenda for social and economic justice and for peace.

No, Ron Brown is no Jesse Jackson — although he got his job thanks to Jesse, and to me, and to the Black community, which responded with passionate enthusiasm to the progressive agenda for which we both stood. But Ron Brown stands opposed to that agenda. He is already talking about reneging on the rules changes that Reverend Jackson negotiated with Michael

Dukakis. The Democrats want to appear as if they're making concessions to the Black community by putting Brown into a visible position of power. But putting a Black face on conservatism does nothing for the Black community. It is just neo-colonialism, Democratic Party style.

This is the answer of the white supremacists in the Democratic Party to the Black conscience. This is their solution to the growing rebellion in the Black community. And in my opinion it is not working.

Last year we saw the first signs of what I believe is a revolutionary trend in the Black community — a mass break with the white supremacist Democratic and Republican parties and the establishment of a Black-led, multi-racial major party that stands for the Black Agenda.

This rebellion on the part of Black voters has stirred an energetic debate over the issue of whether our empowerment can be realized within the Democratic Party, or whether we must exercise an independent option through a new political party which we control.

The debate over the question of Democratic Party vs. independent party routes to Black empowerment has been on the Black political agenda since the 1960s. It began when Malcolm X issued his scathing indictment of Democratic Party hypocrisy towards our people: "You put the Democrats first," he reminded us, "and the Democrats put you last." The debate continued with Dr. Martin Luther King, Jr., who was considering an independent run for national office before his death in 1968. Both of these great leaders were assassinated before their pro-independent perspective could be given organizational expression.

In 1972 the National Black Political Convention met in Gary, Indiana. In his keynote address Richard Hatcher, the mayor of Gary and one of the first Black mayors of a major American city, handed down a passionate indictment of the major parties. He said, "In our infinite patience, we have tried year after year, election after election, to work with the two major political parties. We believed the pledges, believed the platforms, believed the promises, each time hoping they would not again be sold out... hoping... hoping... always hoping.

"We are through believing. We are through hoping. We are through trusting in the two major white American political parties...

"We shall no longer bargain away our support for petty jobs or symbolic offices. If we are to support any political party, the price will now run high — very high... We emphatically reject the role of advisor to the party's governing circles. Advisors are impotent. We are strong. Advisors do not vote on vital ques-

68

3,000 gathered at Atlanta's historic Wheat Street Baptist Church for Black Agenda rally during July 1988 Democratic National Convention. Above, Dr. Fulani speaks before Minister Farrakhan's address.

tions. We must have a vote in every decision which affects the party, Black people and the country.

"No political party which represents the interests of America's giant corporations, rather than the urgent needs of the people, may enlist Black political power in its support... Hereafter, every political party must make up its mind. It cannot represent both the corporations and the people. As the party chooses, so shall we then choose the party.

"We say to the two American political parties: This is their last clear chance; they have had too many already. These are not idle threats...The choice is theirs...Those of us still committed to a political solution may then cross the Rubicon and form a third political movement.

"I for one," Mr. Hatcher concluded, "am willing to give the two major parties one more chance in the year 1972 to redeem themselves but if they fail us — a not unlikely prospect — we must then seriously probe the possibility of a third party movement in this country."

"...now that Black-led independent politics has definitely arrived on the scene, many of those who were only talking independence are all riled up."

But despite those eloquent and truthful words, the convention ultimately rejected the option of building an independent Black party; instead they opted for the strategy of increasing the number of Black elected officials and focused their efforts on the Democratic Party. Folks associated with the Convention did go on to form the National Black Independent Political Party — NBIPP — but while NBIPP was committed in theory to a national Black party, it was unsuccessful in realizing that goal.

When the current wave of Black-led electoral activism — the Rainbow movement — began to emerge in the early 1980s it developed both inside and outside the Democratic Party. In 1981, when the African American community and the labor movement in New York City came together to field a candidate against Mayor Ed Koch, we ran our Dump Koch candidate — Frank Barbaro — both in the Democratic primary and as an independent in the general election on the Unity Party line. And Harold Washington's successful effort to become mayor of Chicago was also fueled by an independent coalition that managed to gain control — if only temporarily — of the local Democratic Party.

On the national level Reverend Jackson's Rainbow Coalition located itself inside the Democratic Party, but it has been accompanied from the beginning by an independent Rainbow movement, spearheaded by the New Alliance Party. As the first African American and the first woman ever to be on the ballot in every state, my independent Presidential candidacy set the stage for the Black rebellion and for the intensified dialogue on our relationship to the Democratic Party that has followed in the wake of the rebellion.

Much of the debate has been honest, principled, and serious. Folks have a lot of questions about leaving the Democratic Party. For example during the campaign I was often asked whether my candidacy wasn't really helping George Bush because I was out to Dump the Duke! I told people that No, I wasn't helping Bush; I was projecting a strategy whereby the Black community could exercise political power by going independent and teaching the Democrats that we would not be taken for granted, that we would not allow our leaders to be mistreated, and that we would not allow the Black Agenda to be sacrificed on the almighty altar of elect-a-Democrat-because-that-would-be-better-than-electing-a-Republican. The Democrats and the Republicans together have given us, the Black people of this country and our sisters and brothers of color, nothing but racism, poverty and war. When Minister Louis Farrakhan and I appeared together at the Black Agenda conference in Atlanta last July, he told our people not to be intimidated by the Democrats' pleas that we support the lesser of two evils. He said the two parties are just like Lucifer and Satan — we catch hell either way!

So a lot of the debate has been serious. But there have also been Black leaders who depend on the Democratic Party for their own advancement — for positions, for status, and for money — and they have warned us away from independent politics. Sometimes they've said it in so many words; sometimes they've beaten around the bush. Black people aren't ready, they say; it's a good idea, but the time isn't right, they say; we'll only hurt ourselves, they say. But it all comes down to the same thing: play it safe, vote for the lesser-of-two-evils Democratic Party because the Republicans are more evil. Whatever they say, though, the folks who are saying it mean: please don't get me in trouble with the Democrats by voting independent: my good job, my fine house, my social connections depend on it.

Now not only independent politics in general, but the New Alliance Party in particular, is very controversial. Why? Well, leaving the rumors aside — the rumors that NAP is a cult, that I am brainwashed or a brainwasher, that NAP isn't really Black-led, that NAP is really a front for the neo-fascist fanatic Lyndon LaRouche, and the rest of the nonsense — there's a very simple explanation. The fact is that a lot of folks have been talking about the need for independent politics for a long, long time. But now that Black-led independent politics has definitely arrived on the scene, many of those who were only talking independence are all riled up. You see, to them it was just rhetoric. They used the language of independence for their own purposes: to prove to us that they were militant. They just never meant it to be taken seriously.

But independent politics is very serious, and the talkers are scared! Because in 1989 independent politics isn't just talk. It's real — a real movement that's underway in America, and those who make their living from keeping the Black community quiet, under control and in the Democratic Party fold are in for a rude awakening.

A few weeks ago I appeared on *Tony Brown's Journal* with Dr.

Ron Walters, a professor of political science at Howard University in Washington, DC who was Reverend Jackson's campaign manager in 1984 and a key adviser to the 1988 Jackson campaign. The show, which aired all over the country, was entitled "Who's Who On the American Left?" Dr. Walters spent the entire time throwing all kinds of accusations around. He said that I was a puppet of Jews; he said that I was not credible. And he said, "As far as I'm concerned, 2% of the Black vote is nothing." Well, as far as I'm concerned, 150,000 Black folks pulling the lever for an independent Black woman ain't "nothing"! So why is Dr. Walters trying to dismiss the significance of my campaign for the Presidency, and the significance of my results? Because he and other Black leaders have to cover over the fact that coming out of the 1972 Gary convention, they over-committed the Black community to the Democratic Party.

My concern in building the New Alliance Party is that the Black community must continue to lead the independent political movement that is now underway in America. We cannot afford to stand on the sidelines giving away our votes to Jesse Jackson the Democrat while the white supremacists take over the Democratic Party and turn it into an all-too-loyal opposition party in name only — to the Republicans.

The fact is that the major parties — beholden as they are to white corporate America — have made it very clear that they neither have nor want a conscience. If the Republicans and Democrats who make public policy at every level — from the county courthouses and city halls to the state legislatures and the governors' mansions to Congress and the White House — had a conscience then hundreds of thousands of our people would not be living on the streets and in the bus stations because the professional politicians are not sufficiently concerned to guarantee that they have somewhere decent to sleep. Tens of thousands of our people would not be dying of AIDS because the politicians are not sufficiently concerned to mobilize a national effort to find a cure. The right of all women to choose a safe abortion would not be in jeopardy because the fanatic far right-ers are on a rampage and their friends in high places are too cowardly to stand up to them. South African apartheid, the reign of terror against the Palestinians, the contra thugs in Nicaragua and their counterparts in Angola — Jonas Savimbi's UNITA forces — would not be receiving the financial, diplomatic and military backing of the United States because the politicians prefer fascism to socialism as a solution to poverty and repression.

No, the Democrats — like the Republicans — have no use

Dr. Fulani with New Alliance Party chapter builders. From left, Gay Johnson, Jeremiah Duboff, Ola Mae Williams, Domingo "Tato" Losado, Janine Carpenter, NAP executive board member Dr. Fred Newman, Alvaader Frazier, Esq., James Mangia, Lourdes Perez and William Sherman.

for the Black conscience. They walk all over it. What the servants of wealth recognize is power, not conscience. That is why there is a growing recognition that we must have an independent option. What are some of the signs that independent politics is sweeping the country? In Chicago, Alderman Timothy Evans withdrew from the Democratic Party primary in order to run for mayor as an independent. His supporters easily succeeded in gathering the 25,000 signatures needed to put Evans on the ballot as the candidate of the Harold Washington Party. The newly created party was named for Chicago's first Black mayor, who died nearly a year and a half ago.

Although 17 candidates had announced that they were running for mayor of Chicago, from the beginning the race came down to Evans, acting Mayor Eugene Sawyer — who like Evans is Black — and the white machine candidate Richard Daley, whose iron-fisted, notoriously racist father ran Chicago for decades.

Until Tim Evans decided that he would run independent, the likely outcome of the primary was that he would split the Black vote with Sawyer and thus return the Daley dynasty to City Hall. By opening up the independent road, Timothy Evans has given the African American community and its allies in the Chicago Rainbow another way toward their empowerment.

Alderman Evans' campaign is an example of the "inside/outside" tactic which I called "Two Roads Are Better Than One." Eugene Sawyer is now the Black community's shot within the

> **"The major parties — beholden as they are to white corporate America — have made it very clear that they neither have nor want a conscience."**

Democratic Party — as Jesse Jackson was on the national level in '88 — and Evans is the independent backup in the very likely event that Daley becomes the Democratic nominee. That's the kind of Black empowerment strategy that can put the white supremacist Democratic Party on the defensive—which is exactly where it belongs.

There are other, urgent appeals for independent politics coming directly out of the Black community. I'm sure you followed closely, as I did, the news of what the white corporate-owned media called the "riot" in Miami last month. That upsurge of rage at yet another instance of the wanton police murder of young Black men was not a "riot" but the latest battle in a war being fought by poor people facing an occupation army and who — like the Palestinians — have nothing else for weapons except stones and bottles. All the Black Democrats from Tallahassee, the Florida state capital, to Washington, DC have not been able or willing to stop the rampage of poverty and police violence against the people of Overtown and Liberty City.

That outbreak of furious anger against the rampant and officially sanctioned brutality that is endemic in America — from East New York to East Los Angeles, Minneapolis to Miami — represented, I believe, a growing recognition on the part of the poor and working class Black community that while the Black middle class has been assimilated into the mainstream of American economic, political and social life, with all the attendant privileges of such assimilation, poor Black people are not ever going to make it unless there is a radical restructuring of the system. They recognize that without such fundamental change, the ghetto is not only our past and present, it is our future.

I was interviewed on Miami radio while the "riot" was going on and I told our Black sisters and brothers there that our response to police brutality, racism, and poverty must be to make the break with a political system that engenders hopelessness. We know that the Republican Party is no friend to the Black community. And the truth is that Democratic Party reforms have done virtually nothing for our people. That is why

I believe we have to have our own political party that represents and fights for the Black Agenda and the Rainbow social vision. I invite you to join me.

A TRIBUTE TO REVEREND AL SHARPTON

Reverend Al Sharpton is deeply respected in the African American working class community; our people know that he is not afraid to stand up to the white Powers That Be on our behalf. For exactly the same reason many Black leaders are wary of Reverend Sharpton, just as they are wary of Minister Louis Farrakhan. Establishment Black leaders are used to being told — from the columns of the white corporate-owned media, from the official pronouncements of the white Democratic Party leadership, from the pulpits of "liberal" white clergymen — who is legitimate, who is acceptable, who among us is "a credit to our race" AND WHO IS NOT. They are used to being told which leaders it is alright to be close to, and which to avoid — or denounce.

Like Minister Farrakhan, Al Sharpton is an illegitimate Black leader in the eyes of the Powers That Be. Why do they hate him? The explanation is simple: he doesn't dance to their tune. His loyalty is, first and foremost, to the Black community. For this "crime," Reverend Sharpton has come under heavy attack from the white political and media establishments in New York. Governor Mario Cuomo, "Mr. Democratic Party liberal," has said publicly that he wishes Reverend Sharpton were dead. He is currently being prosecuted in the courts as a "tax evader." The corporate media, conducting a campaign of vilification against him, have "exposed" Reverend Sharpton as a police informant and echoed the slander that he is an "anti-Semite."

Phony exposes are part of a long tradition in the effort to intimidate and punish independent Black leaders. They did it to Marcus Garvey. They did it to Adam Clayton Powell. They did it to Dr. Martin Luther King, Jr. and to Malcolm and to the Black Panthers. They are doing it to Minister Farrakhan. The purpose of such tactics is to scare Black leaders into silence and inaction. If that doesn't work, the lies and slander prepare the way for violence...

Those Black leaders who crave legitimacy (and the privileges that come from it) have kept their distance from Reverend Sharpton — as they do from Minister Farrakhan — in order not to be tarred by the same brush. They have refused to stand up with him and for him. Some of them have even fallen for the divide-and-conquer tactics that were used in the past to destroy the Black liberation movement by pitting Black leaders against one another; they have joined in the chorus of ridicule and repudiation, to establish their own credentials as "respectable" and "trustworthy" Black leaders.

Through all of this Al Sharpton has stood by his principles and by our people. He has not become less militant or less outspoken — just the opposite. The Black working class knows who he is, loves him for it, and follows where he leads. An illegitimate "troublemaker" to the Powers That Be, Al Sharpton is a working class hero in the eyes of our people.

PHOTO BY: MICHAEL KLEIN

The Reverend Al Sharpton, Emmy Gay, managing director of the Castillo Cultural Center, Dr. Fred Newman and Fulani at screening of *Fulani!* show at Castillo Cultural Center, March 1990.

Most recently, Reverend Sharpton led thousands of young Black people into the streets of New York City to express their revolutionary outrage over the lynch mob-style murder of yet another Black child, Yusuf Hawkins.

Over the years Reverend Sharpton and I have worked closely together. In March of 1987 I joined him in a march on the state capital in Albany to protest the rising tide of racial violence in which Black people — young men like Michael Stewart, Nicholas Bartlett and Michael Griffith, as well as grandmothers like Eleanor Bumpurs — were drowning, and to demand that the state legislature make the racially motivated murder of Blacks and Latinos carry a mandatory life sentence.

On Memorial Day of that year, we were marching together again — this time down Eastern Parkway in Brooklyn — to protest the murder of a 21 year old Black man by a white police officer.

Together we raised our voices to demand justice for our young sister Tawana Brawley, who was driven out of New York as if she were a criminal — when in fact she was the victim of a gang of racists and rapists.

When I brought 5,000 people to Atlanta last summer to demonstrate our support for Reverend Jesse Jackson and my "Two Roads Are Better Than One" plan outside the Democratic Party nominating convention, Reverend Sharpton and busloads of his supporters were there with us.

And when I was not allowed to participate in the nationally televised Presidential debates last fall, Reverend Sharpton — who endorsed my independent candidacy for President of the United States — came to Winston-Salem, North Carolina to lead the protest against my exclusion.

Now he is demanding that I be included in New York's mayoral candidate debates — to guarantee that our people have a voice in the upcoming election.

I am very proud to be a Black leader who follows the leadership of Reverend Al Sharpton. He is an independent Black leader who refuses to sell himself to the Powers That Be — because he has given himself to the Black working class.

SPEAKING FOR BLACK AND PUERTO RICAN UNITY

During the 1989 New York City municipal elections, Dr. Fulani underscored the importance of Black and Puerto Rican unity, a cornerstone of the New Alliance Party since its birth in the South Bronx in 1979. In that election New Alliance Party candidate Pedro Espada, a grassroots Puerto Rican leader from the South Bronx, polled 42% of the vote in a near upset of the racialistic Bronx Democratic Party organization and became a political "role model" for insurgent Democrats all over the country.

Good evening, sisters and brothers. I am very glad to have this opportunity to share with you the latest developments in the struggle for Black and Puerto Rican empowerment in the upcoming elections.

As many of you know several weeks ago David Dinkins filed a "declination of designation" repudiating the 25,000 signatures that were gathered by the Coalition for a Progressive New York and the New Alliance Party to help put him on the ballot in the Democratic Party primary on September 12. It was the first time in the history of this city that a candidate rejected only a portion of the signatures collected on his behalf. In this case most of those signatures came from the African American and Puerto Rican communities — the very communities that Mr. Dinkins is counting on to deliver the Democratic Party nomination to him.

Mr. Dinkins thus handed City Councilman Rafael Castaneira Colon, a man who has been ripping off the people of the South Bronx for decades, an opportunity to force his only opponent in the primary, Mr. Pedro Espada, off the ballot. Colon argued that Mr. Dinkins' repudiation of the signatures meant that they didn't count for Mr. Espada, whose name appeared on the same nominating petitions. Yesterday afternoon a Bronx Supreme Court judge ruled.

Why did Mr. Dinkins decide to dump those 25,000 signatures? And why did he refuse to change his mind even after he became aware that Colon (who, by the way, has just endorsed Dinkins) and his boss Ramon Velez were using the "declination of designation" to maintain their corrupt hold on the Councilmanic seat? Is this what David Dinkins means when he says he is the candidate of Black and Puerto Rican unity? What was the problem with those NAP gathered signatures?

Mr. Dinkins said in court that he didn't know anything about it. But you know that can't be true! Someone told Dinkins that if he didn't publicly disassociate himself from NAP he'd forfeit their support. And he bowed to the pressure. He made a deal. Mr. Dinkins made a deal because the Powers That Be told him he shouldn't have anything to do with me or with NAP. And if Colon reaped the benefits while the Puerto Rican people of the 11th Councilmanic District paid the price, David Dinkins was prepared to go along. That says something about who David Dinkins is and where his loyalty lies. In the case of Pedro Espada, it says a lot about how much David Dinkins cares about Black and Puerto Rican unity.

The fact is that NAP has become *the* issue in the upcoming elections. Because where the major party politicians stand on this Black-led, multi-racial, independent party tells you where they stand on democracy, where they stand on empowerment and where they stand on the *people* of New York.

You see, NAP is supported by tens of thousands of people —

Dr. Fulani campaigns for governor in the South Bronx with Pedro Espada and Sandra Love, New Alliance Party-backed Democratic Party district leaders, and her running mate Ivonne Vazquez, NAP candidate for lieutenant governor.

African American people, Latino people, Native American people, progressive white people, lesbians and gays. Last year NAP made history when I became the first woman and the first African American Presidential candidate ever to be on the ballot in every state and the District of Columbia. Last year two percent of the national Black vote and two percent of the national gay vote went to me, the independent New Alliance Party candidate. There is *no reason* for anyone who calls himself or herself pro-Black, pro-Puerto Rican, or progressive to attack such an independent party — *unless* they've made a deal. Unless they've bowed to pressure by the machine. And if they've made that kind of deal, then we have the right to know what other deals they're making behind the backs of our people.

In fact you *can't* call yourself pro-Black (or pro-Puerto Rican or progressive) and be anti-NAP. Now I am not saying that everyone has to support NAP. I'm not saying that everyone has to agree with NAP. I'm saying that there is a principled position to take regarding this people-instead-of-profits party on the part of those who *aren't* NAP supporters. Reverend Jesse Jackson is a Democrat, not an independent. He doesn't agree with independent politics. During the 1988 campaign he came under heavy pressure to repudiate me. But he refused to do so. He has consistently acted with respect towards NAP because of what our

Fulani at Puerto Rican Day Parade, New York City, June 1990. Dr. Rafael Mendez is at left.

party stands for and what we are building.

I regret to say that Mr. Dinkins and a number of other members of the Black and Puerto Rican political establishment have not done so. Our people deserve better — much, much better — than that. And the New Alliance Party is here to see that they get it. The issue is democracy. Our message to Mr. Dinkins and the rest of the dealmakers is this: if you don't want a Black-led, multi-racial progressive party included in the political life of the people of this city, our communities demand to know the reason why!

As you know, the Coalition for a Progressive New York, which has come together around my independent campaign, and I are supporting Mr. Dinkins in the primary. If he wins we will do everything we can to see that he becomes the next mayor. We believe that an African American with a history as a reformer would make a better mayor for all the people of New York than an anti-poor, anti-labor, racist bully like Ed Koch or any of the other professional wheelers and dealers in the race.

But if Mr. Dinkins does not get the nomination, I will be on the ballot in November on the NAP line to give our people a voice, an independent voice, a Black-and-Puerto Rican-unity voice, in this election. I believe that Black leaders need to *lead*;

they need to go into the Puerto Rican community and the progressive white community speaking out on behalf of the Black Agenda for social and economic justice and that our sisters and brothers in those communities will respond. It's not only Black people who have no reason to support leaders who won't lead, who won't fight for the community. Why should *anyone* support a mealymouthed yes-man? After all, if Black leaders are afraid to fight for the Black community, they sure as hell aren't going to fight for anyone else!

As an independent, I am able to raise the life and death issues that are of profound concern to our communities — controversial issues the professional politicians don't want to touch. Issues such as the fight to save Adam Abdul-Hakeem (formerly known as Larry Davis) and Ricardo Burgos, the two young Black men who have become the targets of a murderous police vendetta because they dared to reveal that for years corrupt officers have been recruiting Black and Puerto Rican youth for the drug ring they operate out of the 44th Precinct in the South Bronx and the 34th Precinct in Harlem.

Why is this case so important to us? It is not only that two of our children are in danger of being murdered by vengeful cops — although that danger is very, very real. But it means even more than that. The case of Adam Abdul-Hakeem and Ricardo Burgos embodies those controversial and contentious issues that the professional politicians refuse to touch: police brutality; the epidemic of drugs; the absence of jobs and job training and the collapse of the education system — all of which tell our children that there is no future for them.

As the single mother of two Black children — a daughter, Ainka, just turned 16, and a son, Amani, who is 12 — as a developmental psychologist and as a political activist, I am determined to fight for the future of all of our children.

TAWANA BRAWLEY AND THE CENTRAL PARK JOGGER; DOWN WITH THE DOUBLE STANDARD!

The case of Tawana Brawley was a prime example of the racist double standard that is practiced in America. Tawana was not only gang raped by six white men, some of whom had ties to the local police — she was raped again by the corporate media. The name of this young Black daughter was smeared across the front pages of the country's newspapers and television screens; pictures of her nude body were displayed at random; her family and her supporters — the Reverend Al Sharpton and attorney Alton Maddox — were viciously attacked; millions of words were published and broadcast "proving" that the rape story was a hoax perpetrated by someone who was no better than a slut and habitual liar. There was no anonymity. There was no compassion. And there was no justice.

The case of the Central Park jogger is another perfect example of the double standard at work. It is clear to the African American community — and to every decent-minded person, Black and white, in this country — that the rights of the young Black and Latino men who were rounded up to pay for the crime of violence committed against an affluent white woman (three of them have already been convicted of rape) have been blatantly and viciously violated at every stage by the cops, the courts, and the white corporate-owned media.

Those of us who raise the issue that the constitutional rights of these young men were and are being violated — that they are being railroaded to prison on a one-way track — have been accused of condoning the rape. As the mother of two Black teenagers, a 17 year old Black daughter and a 13 year old Black son, I take both rape and racism very, very seriously. We have to say NO to both!

The double standard is also alive and well in American electoral politics. Unlike white folks, Black people are expected to give our votes loyally to the Democratic Party, year in and year out, without ever getting anything in return.

The Powers That Be in this country use the double standard to keep people divided. It makes some folks think they're better than others just because those who run this country on behalf of white corporate America are prepared to give them a little bit more (more money, more justice, more power) so that they'll keep their mouths shut and fight to keep the ones with less down. But we can't afford to allow ourselves to be manipulated in that way — it's a fool's game.

As the chairperson of the New Alliance Party, and as NAP's candidate for governor of New York this year, who is waging a militant campaign for youth and democracy, I am working day and night to build an independent party which challenges that double standard, tears it down and destroys it.

We are building a party which will not allow women and Blacks to be pitted against one another while the white corporate-owned media — which don't much care how many women are violated or how many men of color are lynched — make big bucks selling rape and racism. A party which will fight to defend the young brothers accused in the Central Park case and the thousands like them who are automatically suspect just because they are Black, or Puerto Rican, or Chicano or Asian or Native American. A party which demands that the Tawana Brawleys of America receive the same respect and justice that white women who have been raped expect (and deserve). A party that is bringing together in a new alliance those that the Powers That Be are so desperate to keep divided. But we're a lot smarter than that.

THE ADL'S PROBLEM: NAP IS NOT "DECEPTIVE" BUT ATTRACTIVE

This past week the Anti-Defamation League of the B'nai B'rith — an organization whose mission is supposedly to monitor anti-Semitism and other forms of bigotry — published its latest attack on the New Alliance Party, Dr. Fred Newman — the progressive Jewish activist who is a dedicated builder of the Black-led independent political movement — and me.

The ADL's 13 page "research report" is called *The New Alliance Party: A Study in Deception.* It is an attempt to smear the independent party that I chair as an anti-Semitic, "far left" cult controlled by Dr. Newman. Some people believe that it is better to ignore such vicious (and stupid) attacks. But I think it is important to pay very close attention to what the ADL is saying — because what you see is *not* what you get.

While pretending to be concerned about NAP's anti-Semitism, the ADL report reveals that the organization's real problem is the coming together of Blacks and progressives — particularly progressive Jews like Fred Newman — who share a deep and passionate commitment to building the Black-led, working class-wide independent organizations and alliances, such as NAP and Reverend Al Sharpton's United African Movement, that are rising up to lead the fight for radical (meaning real, people's) democracy in this country.

In a section of the report called "Targeting the Black Community," the ADL says that "The NAP... has attempted to forge an alliance with New York radical activist Rev. Al Sharpton..." The implication is that the United African Movement/New Alliance Party coalition is a scheme which hasn't worked out yet. But the fact is that it's very, very real — far too real for the likes of the ADL. Because what the forces of reaction and their agents fear most of all is exactly such an alliance between Blacks and progressives.

"Doggin' Dinkins." Fulani at "Save David's Soul" Rally, Greenwich Village, September 1989.

Together NAP and the UAM have emerged as the organized, grassroots-based pro-democracy opposition to the corrupt and long-entrenched Democratic Party establishment in New York which runs the city in the anti-people interests of the banks and the big landlords. That political establishment is now represented by David Dinkins, New York's first Black mayor, who spent the last days of the campaign advertising the fact that in 1985 he had tried to prevent Minister Louis Farrakhan from speaking in the city. The message was that Dinkins was one of those "good Blacks" who — unlike the outspoken, "uppity" ones such as Minister Farrakhan, Reverend Sharpton and me — deserved the trust of Jewish voters.

Last week Mr. Dinkins and I ran into each other when we were both panelists on the nationally televised TV show *America's Black Forum.* He is still highly annoyed with me because as an independent mayoral candidate last year I dogged him around New York to demand that he be responsive to the concerns of the African American and Puerto Rican voters he was counting on to make him the mayor.

On the show David defended himself against my charge that in his efforts to attract the most racist elements of the Jewish community he had betrayed our people by saying that his repudiation of Louis Farrakhan was a matter of principle — David Dinkins doesn't want this Black people's leader in "his" city! Yet David isn't prepared to acknowledge that my "doggin' Dinkins" campaign was also a matter of principle — I will do whatever is necessary to make him accountable to the African American community (and I won't back off just because he is a "brother").

The ADL's attack on NAP, and the stepped-up campaign by New York's political and legal establishment to harass Reverend Sharpton, comes at a time when the new coalition that we are building together is just coming into existence. It is a dangerous moment for David Dinkins, the anti-democratic, corrupt Democratic Party that runs the city, and the financial Mr. Bigs to whom the professional politicians owe their souls. This coalition represents the coming together of those whom the Powers That Be all over the world *will stop at nothing* to keep apart — people of color and progressives.

From the ADL's vantage point, the problem and the danger is not that the New Alliance Party is "deceptive," but that this Black-led, multi-racial, people-instead-of-profits independent party is ATTRACTIVE to progressive Jews like Fred Newman.

A NEW KIND OF VOTER

In 1990 Dr. Fulani ran for governor of New York State at the head of the New Alliance Party's independent slate of local and statewide candidates. The following is a statement she made to the press during her campaign for youth and democracy.

The African American people of New York State — like the Puerto Rican people and other communities of color — are increasingly outraged at the utter failure of Governor Mario Cuomo and his Democratic Party to respond to the issues and agendas that are of most concern to our people: racial violence and police brutality; joblessness and poverty; the epidemics of AIDS and of homelessness; the failure of the schools and hospitals to meet the needs of our families.

As a political activist, and as a practicing therapist in Harlem, and now as the New Alliance Party's candidate for governor, I am in the communities day in and day out. I hear what

85

folks are saying in the street. And the word is that this is the year to make the statement that a new kind of Black voter is emerging — an independent Black voter who will not vote party line, who will not vote for the Democrats just because "that's what we've always done."

My appeal to the Black electorate, to Puerto Rican voters, to lesbian and gay voters, to rank and file trade unionists, and to all progressive-minded people is that we all need to say NO to Mario Cuomo — and YES to independent politics.

You see, it is not only that Mr. Cuomo and his party have been unresponsive to our communities; they have adopted an adversarial relationship to them. Attorney General Robert Abrams, this state's senior law enforcement official, has used the power and authority of his office to pursue a political vendetta against the Reverend Al Sharpton and attorney Alton Maddox — in my opinion and in the opinion of substantial numbers in the Black community, the pre-eminent civil rights leaders of this generation — because they dared to stand up to him and the rest of the political and judicial establishment first in the case of Howard Beach, and then in the case of Tawana Brawley, to demand justice for the African American community.

Nor is the Black community the only community that has been hurt: the rising tide of police violence against Latinos, gay bashing, AIDS, the givebacks that are being rammed down the throats of organized labor — these have all gone unheeded by our "liberal" governor, who hopes to sweep all this under the rug and present himself as a popular liberal.

Mr. Cuomo, in fact, looks more conservative and unpopular every day. Press reports indicate that he and the three white, male gubernatorial candidates of the Republican, Conservative and Right to Life parties have arranged to debate one another while excluding me, the only African American woman in the race. It is no secret that the Democratic Party, together with the entire spectrum of the state's current ballot status parties, regard Black people and all people of color as not "legitimate" (the word Mr. Cuomo's representative used in defining who was qualified to take part in the debates when he said I wasn't) and "lunatic" (the word the Conservative Party chairman used to describe me).

For these reasons, and because Yusuf Hawkins lies dead and buried and Tawana Brawley has yet to receive the same justice and respect as the Central Park jogger; because the police recruit Black and Latino children to sell drugs for them and not a single elected official — Democrat or Republican, Black, Latino or white — has lifted a finger to do anything about it;

Campaigning in Harlem, Fall 1990

because of all these profound injustices, there is a growing disaffection among all of our people towards the professional politicians of the Democratic Party, from Mario Cuomo in Albany to David Dinkins in New York. And 1990 is the year to express our protest against what they have done, and for what they have not done.

Now I know that before too long our elected Black officials will be out in force to do their job, which is to bring in the Black vote for their boss Mario. But as we approach the dawn of a new century, a new kind of voter is emerging — the independent voter: the independent Black voter, the independent Puerto Rican voter, the independent lesbian and gay voter, the independent labor voter, the independent woman voter. And we are going to create a Black-led, multi-racial, progressive independent ballot status party this election that will change the face of politics in this state — and in this country — forever!

PROUD TO BE IN HISTORY

Good afternoon, and As Salaam Aleikum to my Muslim sisters and brothers. When this Friday evening, October 19th, four of the candidates running for governor of New York State will have a for-whites-only debate, noticeably absent on Friday evening will be the only woman and only African American running for governor of this state. Noticeably absent will be any

87

Press conference where Minister Farrakhan and Reverend Sharpton endorse Dr. Fulani's candidacy for governor of New York, October 1990.

mention or reference to the Black Agenda and the concerns of the Black community for economic and social justice. The Black Agenda is of no interest to Governor Cuomo and the other candidates for governor. It will be ignored. And, like it, I will be locked out, denied access to participation as my people have been and continue to be in this country. This lockout is even more ironic since the leadership of the African American community continues to serve as the conscience of America. And without that leadership, the crisis in America cannot be solved, not the economic, not the social, not the political or spiritual crisis.

The killings will not stop unless Black leadership and the Black community are at the forefront leading the way. This is why I wholeheartedly support Reverend Sharpton's call for us to do whatever we can do to have Minister Farrakhan speak in the city of New York. I am deeply proud and deeply honored to receive the endorsement of these two extraordinary Black leaders, Minister Louis Farrakhan and Reverend Sharpton. It is clear that these brothers have lived their lives involved in a passionate fight for the Black Agenda and that they have fought ruthlessly to free our people from oppression. It is clear to me that all decent people in this country do or will come to recognize the importance of their leadership — the leadership provided by these men, because decent people in America also recognize the fundamentality of the Black struggle against racism and economic oppression if there is to be progressive change at all in this country. It is African Americans who must and who will lead the way in the challenge to the oppression of all oppressed peoples — people who have been and who will continue to be destroyed by a rich white male America, unless there is drastic and dramatic change. So I am honored, I am deeply moved. I am honored to be here with each of them, proud to be in history with my brothers in struggle. I accept this endorsement on my behalf and on behalf of the New Alliance Party, and I promise you it will be used well. Mario Cuomo — look out!

SHA

The following
section contains
excerpts from
the Reverend Al
Sharpton's
speeches and
statements
to the press made
during 1990,
and from his
weekly column,
"The Peoples'
Preacher,"
which began
appearing in the
National Alliance
in March
of 1990 and is
now nationally
syndicated.

RPTON

AL SHARPTON: BLACKS & JEWS FORUM

1990 got underway with an historic conference on "Blacks and Jews in New York City" before a multi-racial audience of 500 people at New York Technical College, which brought together two of the most controversial leaders in the country: the Reverend Al Sharpton, president of the United African Movement, and Dr. Fred Newman, a Jewish Marxist who sits on the national committee of the New Alliance Party which Dr. Lenora Fulani chairs. Dr. Fulani served as the moderator of the forum.

The people who have been talking about Black-Jewish tensions are not the people who are involved in either the Black community's tensions or the Jewish community's tensions. Usually it is they who cause the tensions in both communities.

So it seems rather strange to me that people who spend most of their time creating the tensions with which we all live are the ones who have the audacity to convene the meetings to discuss something as if they would try to really put themselves out of business, which would really ease all of our tensions.

One must look at where we are in New York and I think that Dr. Newman was a lot more kind about where we are than I would be. I think that we are in a worse state then we've ever been because it is one thing to be in trouble and it is another thing to be in trouble and not think you're in trouble. We must not think that we have solved the problem of Blacks and Jews with the election of David Dinkins because, if anything, David Dinkins is an example of the problem more then he is a solution.

If David would take a strong drink of coffee, he would see that the Jews he is coalescing with have no influence over the Jewish community! The fact of the matter is they did deliver the votes they claimed they could deliver. So the first thing that David needs to do is read the election returns and then gather all the Jewish leadership that he was meeting with in the basement of Gracie Mansion and commence beating the hell out of all of them! For that combined effort to result in less then 40% of the Jewish vote means: a) that they are not speaking for anybody, b) that they pulled off the greatest con job ever pulled in progressive politics, and c) that they suspect that Dave Dinkins is a dumb nigger at best, and a con victim in fact. Because if there was a coalition that elected David Dinkins, the majority of the Jewish community did not participate in that coalition.

Let us go back to where the Black-Jewish relationship began in the civil rights movement in the 1960s. It began with honest leadership on both sides that was later pimped by impostors on both sides. There is a frank difference between the Martin

Luther Kings and the Abraham Hesses, who were in the trenches fighting together, and those who now sit on Madison Avenue writing up hit lists on people like Farrakhan and me — and Newman — people who have never been in the trenches in *any* community — including their own. They have not fought for Jewish rights, let alone Black rights. So they're really not opposed to the Black struggle, they are opposed to *struggle,* because they are part of the power elite that controls both communities. But those in the 50s who used redbaiting, they now use "anti-Semitism." If you question anybody who happens to be Jewish, you're now anti-Semitic. What is the case against me for being anti-Semitic? I've never made the statements they've accused Farrakhan of. I'm called "anti-Semitic" because I fought an attorney general who happened to be Jewish over Tawana Brawley. Now how fighting one prosecutor — who happens to be Jewish (before I was born) — makes me anti-Semitic is beyond me. But that is their rationale.

Where did the Black and Jewish split begin? They said that we began fighting over Bakke, affirmative action and quotas. Well, the real progressives in the Jewish community had no problem with those issues. It was those who owned the businesses that used Judaism to cover a profit margin that had the problem with affirmative action and Bakke and quotas. Why do you say that, Sharpton? Because how can one take a Bible and years of slavery and international oppression and use them to justify wholehearted support for the creation of the state of Israel, and then turn around and tell me that you don't believe in favors for oppressed people? How can one support Israel and be against affirmative action unless you are a philosophical acrobat? The whole concept of the state of Israel is based on the philosophy of reparations. So how can a Zionist, if he is really for the state of Israel, turn around to Blacks and say "you should not be compensated for your suffering but we should have a state for our suffering"? And the reason this rationale — or irrationale — is not questioned is because, as Dr. Newman has said, it [Israel] is really not a state created for Jews, it is a military base for the United States government. Because if it was a base for Jews, based on history and based on the promise of a homeland, when has the United States government ever been so concerned that it would invest billions into the reparations of an oppressed people? Nowhere in the history of this nation have we ever invested in helping oppressed people. And how could a nation built as a solution to oppression then go and do business with South Africa, the children of the Nazis who brought the Holocaust on their people in the first place? Botha's dad was the one that was in Germany with Hitler and helped kill the Jews. The philosophical heirs to Hitler are the Bothas who are now killing my people in South Africa and trading every day with the state of Israel.

In New York they tell us we can relax now that we have a Black mayor (who Fred voted for!). But it seems a strange conclusion that we can now rest with the election of Dave Dinkins. When Abe Beame was elected the first Jewish mayor, I didn't see anybody close B'nai B'rith down! Or the Anti-Defamation League. Why are the media saying that we don't need activism because of Dinkins, when they didn't feel that we didn't need these Zionist groups when Beame and Koch were in? Because they understood that the Zionist groups really weren't about fighting for the people. Their real goal is to try and put people to sleep in the name of a Black mayor, rather than to keep people awake to implement an agenda that will help Black people *and* other people.

What they have done is to move key Zionists into key positions in the name of Black-Jewish unity. So, you now have a Dave Dinkins, who has to denounce *any* Black leader who has a mass base to satisfy some Zionist who has *no* mass base; if they had a mass base, the majority of the Jewish community would have voted for Dinkins.

Now if you're going to have real unity, you must have unity based on everyone's needs being satisfied. You cannot have a good marriage if only one partner in the relationship is satisfied and another is not. That leads to wandering around at night. Because after awhile you will get tired of satisfying your mate and you being left unsatisfied. In the Black community, being that we are at the bottom of the economic and political and social ladder, if we need mass organizers, people that can inspire our people to remain conscious and disciplined, to move toward real liberation, that is not just a pleasure, that is a *need* we have. So how can we be asked to enter into a relationship with another group of people — for the sake of this discussion, enter into a relationship with Jews — if we have to sacrifice the only mass leaders that we have and need? How can we enter a relationship and be told we have to leave Farrakhan, who can draw more Black masses than anybody in the United States tonight? Or you've got to leave Jackson out, or you've got to leave Sharpton out or Fulani out. You already began the breaking of the relationship inherent in your coalition when you make me come to the table having to give up much of what I need in the first place. So David Dinkins may be the first Black mayor in the city, but he's also the first Black mayor in this country who ran on a platform, complete with commercials, denouncing Louis Farrakhan.

Which means that while he fills one need, he robs another need from the Black community. Because he is establishing a precedent: that sellout and bucking and bowing is part of a winning platform. So what does it matter to have a mayor who is of your race if he cannot identify with your agenda, cannot be seen with your leaders, cannot deal with your leaders? What does it matter to have the first Black governor in Virginia, when he's got to be harder on Blacks than his white predecessors were in order to satisfy some Zionist or some WASP slaveholders who want to use him, in a plantation mentality, to cut off the movement and establish a legacy of sellout as the new style of Blacks in American politics? It becomes short term pleasure but long term pain, because telling Black kids that in order to succeed in the world, you've got to go into this new form of Wilder-Dinkins-Bryant Gumbelism, becomes more dangerous than not having a Black in power at all. There is a passage in the Bible — "what profits a man if he gains the world and loses his own soul." What is more important: to have a political position, or to be able to affirm your self respect and your self dignity? If the price for assuming office is my self respect, then the office is not progress, it is regress, and it becomes a trick to get me to give up my dignity, which is what you wanted in the first place.

What is the case to prove that? Very simple. Mr. Dinkins was told to denounce Farrakhan, and he did. Denounce Les Campbell (Jitu Weusi) and he did. Distance from Sharpton, and he did. *Run* from Fulani, and he did. On more than one occasion! And then, distance yourself from Jesse, and he did. Get

PHOTO BY: RICKY FLORES

Minister Farrakhan and Reverend Sharpton lead march in support of Tawana Brawley, Poughkeepsie, New York, 1988.

rid of Tutu, and he almost did, and the list goes on and on. And whenever it was a question he was expected to denounce in the name of unity. But look on the other side of the equation. When the courts overturned the Howard Beach convictions, were the Jewish leadership denouncing *that*? When a Zionist threw eggs at Bishop Tutu at the inauguration, where was the Zionist leadership then? So it's a lopsided thing, where I'll hand you a list every day and you denounce it, but whatever white people do is alright in the name of unity. This is not unity, this is slavery. This is the same old con job that has always been done to us. For a man of the stature of Desmond Tutu not to be accepted and tolerated by progressive people of all races, and to be insulted by some capitalist Zionist is amazing to me.

For Jesse Jackson, who was able to ignite a fire that helped the Dinkins and Wilders in their Democratic Party, to be shunned because of some Zionist agenda is like a baby being born and spitting at his mother. Wilder and Dinkins did not win because they were distant from Jesse, they won with the exact vote that Jesse helped mobilize in the first place! What kind of political and social ingrate are you that you would tell Jesse to get lost. Or when he comes to the inauguration put him so far on the side, that if somebody was speeding over the Brooklyn Bridge and made a right they would have hit Jesse and his wife! But then Ed Koch is treated with all respect, and those we voted *for* were disrespected in the name of unity.

In conclusion, I agree with Dr. Newman's analysis that their idea of unity is really some kind of con game run by the Democratic Party. Because they only talk about unity in terms of votes. They don't talk about unity economically. I told Jack Newfield that if we want real unity, let's not just vote together. Let's open up a Reverend Al's delicatessen. Let's distribute Shabazz knishes! Let's have a real coalition. But when it comes to economic and social entity, you don't talk about coalitions then, because you're really not talking about coalition, you're talking about coercion. It's easier for you to continue this racist, brutal system when a Black man is enslaved to Blacks while they're dying, so you don't have to worry about answering those questions, you up there in Wall Street taking care of your ventures and your businesses.

So now Colin Powell is justifying the invasion of Panama, and Dave Dinkins will justify the next police brutality act, and Lee Brown will be there to justify the next police act, because no one is talking about how, in the middle of Dinkins' election, Howard Beach was overturned, and now they're getting ready to overturn Bensonhurst because Liz Holtzman did a sloppy job on

Reverend Sharpton with Forgotten Youth of Atlantic City, Labor Day, 1990.

the grand jury. No one is talking about that. They're caught up in the euphoria of 'we are together.' Who is together? The people that were separate are still separate. And the Negroes and the Zionists who are together were *always* together, because they were always taking orders from them. They changed their titles, but their role has always been that they're the caretakers of a power structure that is set up to continue the exploitation and the oppression of their own people. If they were *independent* and self-contained, they would stand up like men and women, but since they are not, they have to go with the same policies that Ed just left with. And this is an amazing disgrace and game that progressive people cannot accept.

I don't care if the perpetrator is Black or white, the game is the same. There is no indication to us that the game has changed in New York. And until the game is changed, you can celebrate the changing of the name alone. Because it means nothing to me to change the name of who's going to perpetrate the same game. Blacks and Jews, if we want unity, we have to deal on the basis of each other's needs, and how we can fight to solve each other's needs, and how we can change the power set-up so that *all* people, in their own community, with their own self respect and dignity, can raise their own children with equal protection under the law. That doesn't mean we have to all be hugging and kissing and loving each other. But it means that if you kill my child in Bensonhurst, or if you beat a Jewish child at Brooklyn College, then both races will object. It means that you have the right to economic self-sufficiency and the right to build your own community — and I have the right to build mine. Unless we can build on that level, then we're not talking about unity, we're talking about the same old game; meeting every once in a while as stockbrokers, to review whether or not the game is still working, and then come out to the press and say 'it's Black and Jewish unity' and put up a hypocritical front and tell the hopeless to keep hope alive.

GO TELL IT ON THE MOUNTAIN

As I sat with a multi-national, multi-racial group of progressive activists and watched the premiere of a New York City cable show entitled *Fulani!*, which is the weekly cable show of my comrade Dr. Lenora Fulani, it occurred to me how progressive activists around the country are not demanding and/or using access battles to assure equal access to the media for all ideological persuasions available on the political spectrum.

It is in fact not our privilege but our right to challenge in local markets our white male conservative media moguls to open up the airwaves and the printed word to the populace whose tax dollars pay the salaries of the FCC (look-the-other-way) regulators. This is just not another issue but is in fact a priority, especially when one has to deal with the fact that it is imperative that the proper information be given so there is not just unilateral control by the power elite over the American mind.

The American citizen has tolerated and in some cases embraced the George Bushes and the Ronald Reagans of this world more out of ignorance and lack of exposure than out of a real conservative mentality. I suppose that is why in biblical days the Apostles were told to go tell it on the mountain — because one cannot convert where one doesn't convey a message.

Growing up in the movement I was often taught that you can't teach what you don't know and you can't lead where you don't go, so I urge all progressives to immediately target, in the spirit of *Fulani!*, local cable stations, TV stations, radio stations and newspapers, to demand equal access to our media.

98

Go tell it on the mountain that workers and Blacks and Latinos and gays have the right to be free and treated with equal protection under the law. Go tell it on the mountain that we need investment in our children more than in our military. Go tell it on the mountain that we need not support the drug cartel, militarily and with subsidies, while standing before high school audiences with our mouths dripping the words, "Say No." Go tell it on the mountain: No Justice, No Peace.

NOW THAT WE'VE HEARD FROM THE DONKEY, WHY BE A JACKASS?

In the last several days the "moderate" leadership of the Democratic Party convened in New Orleans to discuss where they are in the party, what they see as the party's failures in the past, and how they intend to chart the party's course for the future. It was appropriate that they had a token liberal, Jesse Jackson, address the crowd. And after hearing from what they termed "all sides of the party," they released their position papers — which sounded more like the platform of George Bush than the position papers of a "liberal" national party. The most resounding theme was in their conclusion: "We believe in equal opportunity but we do not believe in equal results."

This clandestine, racist, sexist, anti-working class position is transparent to anyone — because to predict at the outset that there will not be an equal outcome economically or socially in society is to have everyone adjust to an unfair balance of power, an unfair distribution of wealth and unequal protection under the law. It is reminiscent of the Dixiecrats of the 40s and 50s who now reign as the moderate Democrats of the 90s going into the 21st century.

Make no mistake about it — the Democratic Party has decided that they will not even attempt to pretend to be liberals. They will now compete with the Republican Party over who can be the most fascist, the most racist, the most sexist and the most homophobic. They want to do it openly and arrogantly. For this party, after eight years of Jackson candidacies, after I don't know how many conferences on delegate selection and equal representation, can now be controlled by the strong moderate wing that has taken social inequality as its theme and economic inequality as its goal. Their motto of economic inequality shows us that we don't have a choice between two distinct and separate animals in the Democratic and Republican parties but that we are faced with a choice between two heads of the same dragon. The fact of the matter is that we no longer have the option of staying Democratic or going independent. We've got the option of intelligently being independent or ignorantly submitting to the liberal wing of the Republican Party known as the Democratic National Committee.

To color this conservative reactionaryism is a DNC chairman by the name of Ron Brown, whose main claim to fame thus far in his reign was to support Richard Daley for mayor of Chicago and to announce that Gus Savage would no longer get party funds he never received in the first place. It only goes to show the outright deception that the Democrats rule by and the lack of respect they have for the masses. Ron Brown would probably be arrested if he wasn't on the DNC finance committee recommending who should or shouldn't get money. And he would certainly be charged with grand larceny counts that would embarrass Robert Abrams' counts against me. It is ludicrous to think that Ron Brown could cut Savage off or cut Savage on — just as it is ludicrous to believe that the Democratic Party will tolerate any progressive or maverick, be he clothed in silk suits, dashikis, dungarees or polyester; it really doesn't matter. The independent stand will not be tolerated — regardless of the costume, culture or design.

Already in 1990 the message for 1992 is coming loud and clear from New Orleans: "We're not going to be liberal with you, even rhetorically. It's time to get down to the real nitty-gritty and put the lumpen proletariat in their place, put the masses in their place, put the Blacks and the women and the Asians and the children and the gays and the others in their place. Let them know that we won't sing the song of equal opportunity, that we will not all end up in an equal place at the end." This is the theme of the donkey. You would only be a jackass to follow.

A LETTER WRITTEN BY REVEREND SHARPTON TO MAYOR DAVID DINKINS, DELIVERED TO GRACIE MANSION BY MOSES STEWART, JULY 22, 1990

Dear Mayor Dinkins:

Despite my very public disagreements with you over the past several months, I do feel proud to address you as mayor. Firstly, because for years I was on the forefront of a movement that finally, successfully defeated your predecessor. Secondly, I played a major role in events that many experts

100

Reverend Sharpton with Moses Stewart (left) and Diane Hawkins (far right), parents of Yusuf Hawkins.

admit led to your primary and general election victory. I hasten to warn you though, my friend, that being the first Black mayor has no lasting historic significance if your administration is nothing but a Black version of business-as-usual.

Ask the average Black American who the first Black United States senator was since Reconstruction, and he would not remember Edward Brooke's name. The reason he has become completely forgotten is that he was here for a season and not for a reason.

New York has severe racial problems. Even the polls which have been hitherto suspect have now conceded that race is a major concern among New Yorkers. Despite the claims that African Americans do not agree with Al Sharpton, the fact is that every Black newspaper has consistently supported our movement. And even the questionable CBS/*New York Times* poll released on June 27, 1990 reported that 30% of Blacks see me as New York's Black leader. Though they claim more are

"We are guilty of being ministers who have taken our calling by God seriously."

against me, the fact that one third support anyone is substantial. If one third of registered Democrats supported Cuomo for President, he would announce tomorrow. And those results were released before my acquittal.

Mr. Dinkins, you will not cover over racism by minimizing it, by ducking it, by trying to appoint your friends as leaders or by trying to censor the media. This approach is a bandaid strategy. You must deal with institutional racism and equal protection under the law. You must deal with the players on the field, whether you like them or not. You would do well to rise above yourself for the whole.

Mr. Dinkins, both whites and Blacks voted for you in the hopes that you would deal with the racial polarization question. If you fail, especially if you fail to really try, history will be unkind to you, despite any other achievement.

I write to you from a maximum security cell on Rikers Island. In the cell next to me is the Reverend Timothy Mitchell, pastor of Ebenezer Baptist Church in Queens and a long time civil rights activist. Directly under the tier are housed New York's most notorious criminals; the killer of patrolman Eddie Byrne, and drug dealers. We are here not because we sold dope or shot a policeman. We did not even commit a misdemeanor. We are guilty of being ministers who have taken our calling by God seriously. It is much more beneficial and possible to preach and avoid dealing with the divinity of all humans. Or not deal with the hungry or sheltering the homeless.

Reverend Mitchell and I were tracked down by the zeitgeist which watched the murder of Claude Reese, Clifford Glover, Willie Turks, Michael Stewart, Eleanor Bumpurs, Michael Griffith and Yvonne Smallwood. We watched with utter amazement as the system refused to punish the guilty. After winning the state's first special prosecutor and winning manslaughter convictions, the courts still sent the murderers from Howard Beach home for an appeal.

So we were outraged and rightfully so. We wanted the nation to know about our feelings. We brought a non-violent march to LaGuardia Airport, where the world comes through. We were arrested and are now jailed. I ask you, Mayor Dinkins: What did we do that Dinkins did not do? Or that Paul Robeson did not do? Do you hang up these men's pictures for art or principle? We are paying a price for issues you must deal with. The fact that a white union at Eastern Airlines disrupted the airport for months, joined by the governor and you, and no one was arrested, much less jailed, and we marched for seven minutes, according to the authorities, shows how justice is imbalanced in this city.

I urged you in the case of Bensonhurst and I urge you now, to immediately sit down with a cross section of Black leadership and deal with the issue of racial justice. You can't hide behind blue ribbons and racial harmony slogans that no sane person will disagree with. You must build a real and just judicial system or I see the day under your mayoralty that blood will flow in the streets unlike ever before. I don't endorse violence and I will not participate in it. But its likelihood is real and it is imminent.

I know we have differences but we must rise above them for the good of all. Meet while there are those who want to meet. The day will come when activists will not even want to hear what City Hall has to say.

God has blessed you. You are in a great position to do great harm or great good. History will record you as a great asset or a great liability. I chose the road of activism that has included death threats, indictments, negative press and even jail cells. But history will record that I did my job and did it well. History will write your record as well. I have brought the issue of racial justice to the front burner. It is the government's job to take the pot on the front burner and to produce a meal for all its citizens. That is why tonight you will sleep in Gracie Mansion and I in a small cell on Rikers Island. But I am free for I have done what is right, no matter who disliked it.

Rise up, Mr Dinkins. Let us write history. Mitchell and I do not mind bearing these crosses. It only better prepares us to wear our crowns.

Yours in progress,
Rev. Alfred C. Sharpton

THE NEED FOR A NEW ALLIANCE

In the Spring of 1968 Dr. Martin Luther King Jr. began convening a cross section of different activist groups throughout major American cities to forge a new alliance of interests that would fight poverty, racism and war in the United States.

He seemed somewhat successful in delivering certain persons, such as Dr. Benjamin Spock, along with SNCC, CORE, his own SCLC, as well as peace activists, ecology activists and environmentalists. What was emerging was that Dr. King was no longer

103

going to be limited by the boundaries of the ghetto. He was going to take center stage in the world, stake his claim, and try to preserve the already shaky earth from being destroyed.

We all know that it led to his support for the garbagemen in Memphis, Tennessee — he spoke on their behalf at the Masonic Temple. The night before he was going to lead their march, Dr. King was brutally and savagely assassinated.

Many years later, I am saying that that same alliance — that same new alliance, if you please — is the threat to today's establishment. Because it is the outcasts who, combined together, have the numbers, the collective energy, the collective manpower and the collective truths to do what has never been done before.

The family of Dave Kemp, the Armstrong family and the other families of the 15 year old kids who were shot by the police show that it is time for a new alliance; those who have now taken power are the former activists of the 50s and 60s whose alliances can no longer work because they are no longer participating in those alliances.

So we need to tear down the walls of the opposition. We need to unite, as Dr. King attempted to, the Black, and the Native American and the Latino and the progressive white and the outcast and the rejected and the homeless and people from all walks of life who have endured pain and neglect only because of the lifestyle they choose or the color of the skin they were born with. Yes, it is time for a new alliance that will bring elected officials into office who represent their constituency, not those who go downtown and come back to represent downtown to their constituents.

We need a new alliance. We have produced lawyers who are advocates for justice rather than candidates for judgeships. We need a new alliance with people who sit in the seats of power to share and distribute power with the populace rather than sit up and posture power for photographers and cameramen to exercise their already too large egos at the expense of the masses of the people, who need power exercised to help lighten their loads.

Yes, we need a new alliance similar to the one at Washington Irving High School in Manhattan [where a citywide meeting of the New Alliance Party was held last Friday night]. A new alliance of people, from "niggers" to "faggots," from "spics" to "wops," who can all lose these derogatory titles together so they can rise up in the true meaning of what they are and who they are, based on their own definitions — not having definitions imposed on them by wicked city, state or national administrations who are there to protect the status quo rather than inform and inspire the public, its customers. This new alliance is the promised land that Dr. King saw; this new alliance is the thing that Adam Clayton Powell wanted us to "keep the faith" for until we could get together; this new alliance is the land that Robert Kennedy saw but could not name.

I believe, as I said on the stage at Washington Irving High School the other night, that half the stage represented pain: the mothers of Adam Abdul-Hakeem and Ricardo Burgos and Moses Stewart, the father of Yusuf Hawkins; the other half of the stage represented promise: Fred Newman, Lenora Fulani, Rafael Mendez, Al Sharpton.

Yes, a proper mixture of promise that is linked to pain is the formula for a new alliance where we will never get social amnesia about what has hurt us and we will never get blinded to the new alliance that we must see and that we must make a reality in our own day.

TEANECK UPDATE *Teaneck, New Jersey exploded the night after the April 10 killing of 16 year old Phillip Pannell, Jr. by a white police officer who put a bullet in the back of the young man as he fled with his arms in the air. The murder shattered the myth of Teaneck as a model integrated community, and brought the chant "No Justice, No Peace!" across the George Washington Bridge to Teaneck Road as the community there called on Reverend Sharpton and Dr. Lenora Fulani in their quest for justice. Reverend Sharpton looked at the issues in building a movement for racial justice in Teaneck a month after the murder.*

On Saturday the new convergence of progressive forces that has sent waves of fear throughout New York State and the northeast corridor of this nation took a definite stand against the corrupt legal system of New Jersey and, as importantly, the bought and compromised phony progressive leadership of the same.

Against loud and well-publicized repudiations, 2500 of us marched into Teaneck for a great outpouring of outrage at the lack of justice in the Phillip Pannell case. I remind the reader how Minister Farrakhan, Congressman Savage, attorney Maddox, Dr. Fulani and I were snubbed by the leadership at the wake. This was followed by an incessant outcry on daily TV and newspapers that we not be permitted to come into town, that we not march, that we stay in New York. The mayor himself said, "It would be best for Teaneck if Al Sharpton stayed home."

But despite this outcry of tyranny, despite this rhetoric of fascism that was echoed by some who have masqueraded around as

105

progressives, we saw the need to put justice on the agenda. The fact of the matter is that since Wednesday night's "riot," following a candlelight memorial for Pannell, there has been no protest, no march, no picket, no demonstration of any kind around the issue of this brutal police act. It is not a question of whether Teaneck wanted to support a Sharpton-Maddox-Fulani march or another march; it was a question of whether Teaneck wanted to support a march, since we were the only march in town. The only thing coming close to calling for justice was an impromptu stop through town by the Reverend Jesse Jackson, who, to the surprise of his sponsors, endorsed the march and said that everyone ought to be marching and everyone should come out and, adding insult to injury, called and had a friendly conversation with attorney Maddox and me, in which he emphatically stated that our position of marching and protesting in this situation was correct.

It seems to me that the Black aristocracy of Teaneck and the phony white progressives had already made their deal with the establishment and had already agreed to replace quiet for peace, and to replace cover-up for real investigation. That was the real threat our presence served as we headed that way on Saturday. The fact that there were two or three thousand more people waiting on us than were on the seven busloads we brought showed that they did not speak for the people of Teaneck, who overwhelmingly cheered our arrival and participated in the march, and have subsequently stayed with us throughout the issue of protecting witnesses and the strategy of witnesses' non-cooperation with the prosecutor. It became paramount to us as we marched with the three eyewitnesses leading the march that the case was not of just a family but, as so many times before, the case of a community that is under siege. People need to remember that the policeman did not roll Phillip Pannell over, go in his wallet, check his last name and shoot him because he was named Pannell. He shot him in the back just as policemen have been shooting Black kids all over this country — Oliver Beasley in Los Angeles, McDuffy in Miami, 22 in New York — because they are Black and no one has to pay for shooting Black people in the back.

So therefore it is not a family decision on how we are going to react to a racial assault. It is also of note that the three witnesses have never been contacted by the leadership of the town and have been subjected to night and day threatening phone calls. Mrs. Curry, one of the witnesses, came home to find her door window smashed out with a note, "nigger bitch, you better forget what you know." We immediately secured them and

106

Reverend Sharpton leads march through Teaneck, New Jersey after police murder of 16 year old Phillip Pannell, Jr., April 1990.

demanded that the attorney general reinforce our security of them. We also announced that they will not talk to prosecutors but they will go straight into the grand jury and state their claims and come straight out, because for them to talk to the prosecutor is for him to try and lead them into inconsistent statements or claim he doesn't have enough to go with. Let them tell their story one time to the state grand jury in Trenton and that will lead to the indictment and prosecution of this murderer in a uniform.

Lessons of Teaneck are still being learned, but some early lessons are still being established. And that is that the false civil rights bureaucracy team cannot match those of us who have decided that we will fight rather than switch. We have proven that those who sit in ceremonial titles do not speak for the masses — no, not even in the suburbs, that their following is those Fortune 500 corporate heads and those elected officials who profit from their mediocrity that survives due to their complacency. But there is a new team on the field that will play even into extra innings, and we are just some of the players on that team. We thought that you heard us in Howard Beach, certainly we thought you heard us in Brawley, and maybe we at least got your attention in Bensonhurst. But let's make it clear in Teaneck that some of us would rather die on our feet than keep living on our knees.

BENSONHURST: WHERE ARE THE DECENT PEOPLE?

Less than a year after the killing of Yusuf Hawkins in Bensonhurst ignited a Black revolution on the streets of New York City that swept out the entire old political establishment and installed David Dinkins as mayor, the United African Movement and the New Alliance Party were back on the streets of Bensonhurst to demand that justice be delivered to Yusuf's killers.

By the time readers will have seen this column, the jury hearing the evidence against Joseph Fama and the jury hearing the evidence against Keith Mondello will be headed toward the jury rooms to deliberate the fate of two of the most notorius racists in memory. There are some very serious lessons to be learned from the Bensonhurst matter.

The only question that remains unanswered is whether the family of Yusuf Hawkins will gain anything from his untimely and unprovoked murder. Certainly others have unashamedly gained by design or accident from the blood that spilled from the body of this young man. David Dinkins gained. It was the anger and humiliation of this senseless act that is responsible for him being mayor today. And certainly there are those in radio and TV, not to mention print journalists, who gained by selling newspaper and television stories with the concern of a wrestling promoter and who used the whole unfortunate incident as a way of igniting Blacks who had been ignited too often before to where just getting angry would not now be enough. Certainly the judge — whose now often quotable one-liners will become part of the annals of judicial history long after my body has gone to its grave — has gained.

So the challenge went out to Yusuf Hawkins' parents to find advice and guidance. They stood with the people and chose the people's leaders — Farrakhan, Maddox, Fulani and Sharpton. Grabbed arms with comrades and marched and raised hell, as well as issues, and supported alternatives to the men who hold office today — the independent candidates for the people. Certainly one remembers not long ago while we were being shouted at and called "nigger" and were spat upon how the great phony liberal Bensonhurst State Representative Frank Barbaro joined the others in the *Village Voice* crowd in saying, "Don't condemn all Bensonhurst. There are good people out here. This has nothing to do with racism." Etc.

Well, one must look in retrospect and see how one can seriously make that claim when, first, the anniversary march of Mr. Hawkins' death was threatened to be marred by more violence

"The failure of the Bensonhurst case is the failure of the city of New York to come to grips with racism."

than New York has ever seen. Secondly, we must realize that young Black people are not willing to sit and wait. We've sat for too long and we sat too comfortable. Where are the good people or Bensonhurst? We were told continually, "Don't condemn them all. There are some good people." Where are the good people? They weren't in Teaneck marching with us. We so-called outside agitators. They were not with us when we came out 10,000 strong marching on the former mayor's Greenwich Village apartment demanding justice in the Howard Beach case. They have been absent from every move for justice — from Howard Beach to Tawana Brawley, Bensonhurst to James Brown — every move for justice that has moved New York directly or indirectly. And each time, we can expect to be humiliated beforehand, and they come in later and proclaim *us* crazy for going about the business of making sure Yusuf didn't die unnoticed and didn't die for nothing.

The failure of the Bensonhurst case is the failure of the city of New York to come to grips with racism. The fact of the matter is a lot of Bensonhurst people saw these 30 kids do this vicious act, but none of those decent people will come forward and testify. Tim Minton, the commentator for WABC television, saw what amounted to be a promo bio on me only to ask, "Now can I talk to Moses Stewart first? Can I talk to Diane first?" Eric Shaw of Fox Televison — same thing, same spirit. And the list goes on.

Despite the mirage, despite counting and clapping, despite whatever the press will be saying in the next few days — I want you to reflect on what it means to have these young men standing in court and what it will mean if the court sets them free. Yes, the phony liberal is mad because we have stripped him of his emperor's gown and replaced it with nothing but a crown of thorns which appears to be settling on his head. Yes, the phony liberals are angry because they should have brought peace to the Black community, but instead they send the Black community a more profound and shocking lesson. So we say: if there is no justice, there will be no peace.

We mean that from the innermost parts of our souls. Ours is not a cosmetic march and a cosmetic aftermath press conference. We came out because we're serious. There must be justice *for* every one of us or there can never be peace *from* any. I conclude by saying that Bensonhurst shatters the myth of the "decent white man" wherever he may be. As he finishes reading this analysis and this recollection, he can stand and tell the world what I have just told the world. And others will join us in telling the world that had not the people of Bensonhurst been appeased and treated like a baby with a pacifier, but had they instead been challenged, had they been pressured, to give up all they know, give up all those who saw something, maybe the context would have been created for the decency in Bensonhurst to emerge. But that, apparently, is not Mr. Genecin's intent.

But as Fama and Mondello pack up, ready to go home to wait for the jury, Black America looks across the bridge down the column. Still water runs deep, small voices run close, the army is not around at all. Please contact us so we can give them up to get back to the battlefield because the people of Bensonhurst didn't hear us, but they will hear us now. Because we will say it in a way that won't be forgotten. And that is: before I'll be a slave, I'll be buried in my grave and go home to my Lord and be free.

Mr. Fama and Mr. Mondello think they've beaten the rap and that they're on their way home. Be that as it may, I will be there not only for those who have been killed but for every man and woman who lives — I'll be there. I'll be the guy not saying we must wait and see, not saying we must pray with our mayor, not saying that this doesn't make sense, but saying to Jack Newfield and the other phony liberal aristocracy that you can fool some of the people some of the time, you can fool some of the people all of the time, but you can't fool all of the people all the time.

AN OPEN MEMO TO THE SIDELINE COACHES

While marching in our largest turn-out to date in Bensonhurst on Saturday, we were joined at the sidelines by Assemblyman Frank Barbaro and a sordid group of the phony liberals who have both caused and reinforced the racial double standard of this city. Their purpose in being present on Saturday was to pass out flyers encouraging the citizens of Bensonhurst to refrain from the ugly name-calling and watermelon-throwing and other racist carryings-on that have now become — thanks to our sacrifice — nationally known as the character of this "gorgeous mosaic" city.

Though it was driving rain, and I think that (as opposed to Barbaro) was the reason for most of the streets being empty, it is interesting to note something that Barbaro falsely claimed. At one juncture, I challenged Barbaro to join the line — "come on march with us!" — and I kept this up for about a block. He declined. Then he tells the press that our marches are not multi-racial, and therefore not representative of the whole public, etc., etc.

First — our marches have all been multi-racial. Every march has been recruited by the United African Movement and the New Alliance Party, and has included people of all racial, religious and sexual backgrounds. It's just that when people put on their Al Sharpton shades in the morning to see only what has been put in their minds regarding what I'm about, non-Blacks don't fit into the picture. So it is difficult for them to see what they see; they see what they have already been programmed to perceive.

Secondly, they claim that we do not add to the solution, that we only heighten the problem. As a person who has been involved in the civil rights movement for 22 years, I consider this charge the most asinine of all, because part of the solution is to heighten and expose the problem. You cannot solve a problem that is not apparent. You cannot approach a problem that is not acceptable. You cannot convince society to spend the money or the time to deal with a problem that society does not feel is a crisis. So to accuse us of heightening and enhancing the visibility of a problem is to accuse us of having half the solution done, because as the problem is heightened, and as the problem is publicized, that gives rise to a call for a solution and a call for using whatever funds and legal maneuvers are deemed necessary to deal with this problem.

People in elected office who take no risk at all in walking around the streets of their own community have turned a deaf and immature ear on their constituents who have told them: Enough is enough! This is wrong.

Lastly I observed that Mr. Mayor Dinkins appealed to people to wear a blue ribbon in saluting racial harmony in the city. Mr. Barbaro and his small throng concurred with the mayor. They went so far as tying blue ribbons on the meters where automobiles were parked, and on the lamp posts throughout the neighborhood.

I must go back to something I was told by my mother many years ago, which is that the Bible says you reap what you sow. If you sow watermelon seeds, you will reap watermelon, and if you sow orange seeds, you will reap oranges. Despite the advances of science, we have not learned how to sow grapefruit and reap turnip greens. We still are bound by the reap-what-you-sow process.

"When people put on their Al Sharpton shades in the morning to see only what has been put in their minds regarding what I'm about, non-Blacks don't fit into the picture."

America can blame the Farrakhans, the Sharptons and the Fulanis, but America planted the seeds of racial disharmony and disrespect. They had this warning in Howard Beach, but they didn't heed the warning. The warnings continued through Brawley, through countless police killings, and they did not heed. They kept planting the seed of liberal, phony reaction, of blame the messenger for the message. And their ignorance watered the seed they planted in 1990 and furthered the dichotomy in the community between those who want to be free and those who want to be in another form of slavery.

But we find that there were others — the Moses Stewarts, the Jean Griffiths of this world — the ones who sowed the seeds of revenge, of protest, of indignation, of *outrage*. And they are the ones who sowed the Al Sharptons and the Lenora Fulanis, the masses who walk through Bensonhurst and walk through Howard Beach and walk wherever necessary.

They are the ones — and the only ones — who have the potential for building a *real* gorgeous mosaic, because they learned the difference between co-option and coalition. Between coming together and being placed together by various and different sponsors. They learned the fact that every race, whether or not it is free, has its own cultural expression, its own social dynamic, that does not have to be sacrificed in the name of "Let's come together." They all should be brought together to the table so people can understand each other's feelings, cultures, and concerns — can understand what each other is saying.

The Barbaros of this world should know that America's future is not in a blue ribbon, but in these people's clenched fists, because it is their defiance of phony liberalism, their defiance of appeasing victims rather than giving them justice, that has preserved this country from major violence.

So let the word go forth to the Barbaros and the Dinkins' of this world that sideline quarterbacking doesn't win the game, or even score. You need to get in it to win it. The answer to a murder is not harmony — the answer is justice.

There is a gentleman of Jewish heritage named Simon Weisenthal who has become internationally respected as the one who chases former Nazi war criminals and brings them to justice. Weisenthal does not adopt the Dinkins-Barbaro tactic of locating former Nazi war criminals and dragging them into a church (or synagogue) to have a harmony rally for them before setting them free and giving them a blue ribbon to celebrate their continued savagery of the human race. Why should I be expected to be any less concerned about the abuse and executions endured by my people?

There is, Mr. Dinkins, a multi-racial march on the streets of New York, a movement of people from all political and sexual backgrounds. There is a mosaic in its developmental stages that will indeed be gorgeous, but it is not the one that you are leading, and not the one that Barbaro led; it is the one that y'all have disdained and looked at with resentment, and looked at with fear, and looked at with eyes of hatred, because you realize that the *real* march, the *real* mosaic, that is happening among us, the real people, will only be the due of those phony liberals who have survived off a patronage system as bloodsuckers of the poor and not as liberators of the downtrodden.

But quiet steps get closer now. We are on the move. We are awakened and we will never sleep again. We must reach for our goal of total liberation. It is in our grasp, and we can only hold our balance as we stretch our toes.

IT IS THEIR PHONYISM THAT HAS MADE US NECESSARY

In his May 17 column, Reverend Sharpton responded to an article in the People's Daily World, *the newspaper of the Communist Party USA, attacking his role and the role of the United African Movement/New Alliance Party coalition in the Teaneck case.*

As hundreds of progressives — African Americans, Latinos, and whites — marched with the eyewitnesses to the murder of Phillip Pannell, Jr. through New Jersey's state capital of Trenton I was handed an article that appeared in the Communist Party paper [the *People's Daily World*-Ed.]. Mr. Ron Johnson, the writer, raised certain questions and/or criticisms of my column, "Teaneck — an insider's view." I rarely in life stop to answer criticisms or questions. But this was so humorous and flattering that I thought I would share with our readers my response as I read Mr. Johnson's diatribe.

Firstly I was glad to see that some members of the phony left did have enough intelligence to buy the *Alliance* newspaper and read my article, because if they would make that a habit they might learn something. Too often they are caught on the wrong side of a fight, and that is behind it rather than in front of it. I think it is appropriate for them to listen to people who are involved on the front lines rather than listening to themselves scream about a front line that they never participate in.

It is very strange to me that Mr. Johnson and his paper would take a posture defending the establishment bourgeois leadership against grassroots challengers. Mr. Johnson seems very clearly in his article to pit Reverend Jesse Jackson against me, saying that Reverend Jackson had come into Teaneck, had met with the leadership in town and met with the governor and met with the elected officials and operated collectively. I came in at the invitation of eyewitnesses and worked with the students at the United African Youth Movement and the Black students at Fairleigh Dickinson University and other lumpen proletariat groups.

One wonders whether Mr. Johnson is just a regular Democrat — he seems to feel the legitimate constituency is the petit bourgeoisie and not the masses one would assume that he at least rhetorically would represent.

Secondly, it seems that Mr. Johnson's information is at best in want of an update. He said that Reverend Jackson met with leaders at the Methodist Church and came out in a solid front with the Pannell family. The fact of the matter is that Reverend Jackson met with several groups, including representatives of mine, the United African Movement, and of the young people who invited me to town. And he very clearly came out of that meeting endorsing the march that Mr. Johnson and the petit bourgeois leadership had denounced. He told me in a telephone conversation that he felt a march was in order because there was no viable or visible protest going on around the Pannell killing.

It may also interest our corporate communist that the Pannell family has reached out to us and in fact the uncle of Pannell marched with us in Trenton. Yusuf Hawkins' father, Mr. Moses Stewart, has talked to the Pannell family, who said that they were not aware at all that they were quoted as having denounced us and that they were in full support of any nonviolent aggressive action that would keep this tragedy in the public's mind until justice can be done. And they were appreciative that we had put protection around the eyewitnesses. I hate to disturb Mr. Johnson, but the key to the case is the eyewitnesses, not just the bereaved family, because the eyewitnesses are the only ones who can establish the police murderer. I'm not surprised that is not known in the corridors of corporate commu-

114

Reverend Sharpton marches in Bushwick, Brooklyn with family of Jose Luis Lebron, shot in the back by police, February 1990.

nism since they do not fight cases, or stand by families or eye-witnesses; they only engage in sideline sniping and rhetorical masturbation.

I might also add that we had an extended meeting with Reverend Jackson just last Saturday at which Reverend Jackson, Mr. Stewart and I agreed on several things. Among them is that a direct action strategy is necessary; appeasing the enemy is unnecessary and all types of ceremonial posing in the midst of outright murders is absolutely counterproductive and counter-revolutionary.

One must question why a leftist columnist and a leftist paper would take this position. The answer is very simple. There has been a serious threat to the white left with the emergence of strong nationalist leadership that does not take orders from them, that doesn't jump when they say jump, that doesn't respond when they yell at you with their patronizing slogans, that demands to think for itself and come up with solutions and analyses that work in the present day. These white leftists are no different from their capitalist twin brothers and sisters. They see Blacks and Latinos — and yes, even lumpen proletariat whites — as their servants as opposed to their comrades. And if you question them you are an uppity nigger and divisive and a rab-ble rouser and all the other things that are slogans not only of the *New York Post*, but of the communist newspaper as well.

I would suggest that we take a signal from this article that the same people who are offended by us on the right are offended by us on the phony left. It is their phonyism that has made us necessary in the first place. They have not embraced, worked for, serviced or helped the Pannell family or the eyewitnesses. So why would they enter the argument to try to make hay from a division that has been repaired and worked out if not to grab some mindless people in the middle who would listen to rhetoricians on the outside who never had the courage to bring their bodies on the inside.

These are the same people who criticize the Farrakhans, the Fulanis, the Maddoxes, and who always have a book full of criticisms for me. What you will never see in their book is a schedule of tending to the needs of people or standing up on an issue or putting their bodies on the line or being persecuted and prosecuted by the legal system. You will never see them do anything but look for weaknesses and criticisms and the opportunity to take cheap shots, and try to establish their movement by negating other movements. The negation of a movement is not the creation of your own. The only way to have a movement is to move and to really be on target and to really deal with the issues.

So I would suggest that the Johnsons of the world continue to read "The Peoples' Preacher" and the rest of the articles in this paper. The only thing you have to lose is your armchair revolutionary status. You might find your legs and march with the real people's movement sooner or later.

MANDELA

As we approach a weekend in which the nation will celebrate the tour of Nelson Mandela, beginning in New York, ending in Oakland, before I could get into the spirit of celebration I received a notice from the first department of the New York appellate court telling me to surrender my body to the authorities on June 20. On the day Nelson Mandela arrives in America, I am supposed to begin serving a 15 day jail term for the grievous crime of protesting racism at LaGuardia airport three years ago.

If it was not so sickening, it would almost be comical to show the obvious desire by those in authority to remove me from the streets during Mandela's visit and to disrupt my bogus criminal trial — which ironically the prosecution rests on the 19th of June, the day before I'm supposed to start the sentence, when I need to be talking to defense witnesses and helping to prepare them for testimony. How do you celebrate and congratulate and even raise and praise an international revolutionary while incarcerating one who epitomizes the same values on your domestic

116

scene? It seems to me the height of hypocrisy for Mayor Dinkins to lead the delegation welcoming Mandela while he joins New York State Attorney General Robert Abrams and Governor Mario Cuomo in leading the posse that's trying to destroy me, Alton Maddox, Lenora Fulani and other progressive leaders.

In 10 weeks of trial we have witnessed the lawyer suspended — now the defendant is ordered to be incarcerated and at the same time put under police protection because of threats against me. I guess the new solution to threats is to take you off the street and put you in the middle of the population of murderers and thugs. Again, it would be comical if it was not so serious.

If Mandela will represent anything in history it will be the consistent, loyal dedication to the principles of freedom for his people and the commitment to uphold those principles that he felt were necessary for freedom at all costs. History will record Nelson Mandela, and rightfully so. It's been 27 long years in jail to stand by a principle that is the most redeeming principle in the human family, and that is the principle of freedom and justice for all people. For that he ought to be regarded among the greatest of men of his day.

However, Mr. Mandela does not monopolize history because that history is being emulated all over the world. People in Nicaragua, people elsewhere in Central America, in Palestine, yes, people in the cities of the United States, have also tried to rise to the occasion. Freedom and justice are uncompromising rights. People are willing to pay whatever price is necessary to assume our freedom and to achieve parity and justice. Therefore, Mr. Mandela ought to be careful as he tours the United States that he not be put in the hands of the oppressors but that he grab the hands of the oppressed and that he seek out those who have sought out the same spirit that made him great. Nelson Mandela should not tarnish his symbol nor his image by running with those who are instituters of apartheid American-style while they hypocritically help him condemn apartheid South African-style.

I recall not long ago helping to convince Don King, the fight promoter, to stop any of his fighters from going to South Africa. It would cost him millions of dollars but he rose to that occasion. I remember sitting with James Brown when he flatly turned down millions of dollars to play Sun City. I remember participating in protests against Millie Jackson and Stephanie Mills for breaking the barrier to performing in South Africa against the will of the ANC and the freedom fighters of that land.

We paid a price, Brother Nelson, to make sure that you had a

117

climate conducive for change. And though you still have a long way to go, because your people are not free, our people paid a little of the price to bring you thus far. Therefore, you should not come to America and run with those who offend us and be saluted by those who uphold American apartheid and who would not challenge anybody, including themselves, not to invest in the financial benefits of the South African regime which holds you and your people in bondage.

Yes, Nelson, it can be a great visit. It's fine that you're visiting the youth at Boys High. It is fine that you are visiting some of the urban centers. But what would be even greater is for you to make a statement on these shores to the first cousins of both Botha and DeKlerk that everywhere in the world there will be no peace until there's justice. And the same spirit that has sustained you for 27 years will sustain those here who fight those racists, those capitalists, those outright killers that control these United States. It would be a great day if you told Pharaoh to Pharaoh's face to let my people go. Then you would not only be Mandela to South Africa, you'd be Moses all over the world.

DESPITE THE DARKNESS, THE LIGHT OF LIBERATION

In March of 1960, a flamboyant progressive political independent walked into a lower Manhattan courtroom accused of tax evasion, accused of using his political operation for personal profit, but really accused of being independent, progressive, Black and not staying in his place. His name was Adam Clayton Powell; the case was United States vs. Powell.

Thirty years later to the month, just a few blocks up in lower Manhattan, I walked into court accused of almost the same crimes for the very same reasons. And if one would study the gap between Adam and Al, one would find all of the glory and all of the shame of Black leadership in this country. The fact of the matter is that in the last 30 years there has been an overt attempt by the system to coopt all Black leadership and to eradicate independent leadership by using the courts, character assassination, vicious media, or outright assassination.

It is ironic that throughout my life, my political hero from age 12 became Adam Powell. My political style has been shaped by my admiration for him, because it was Adam Powell who stood up in the 30s and the 40s and the 50s — alone — teaching the North civil disobedience, boycotts, teaching northern Black leaders how to accumulate power, and then to use power for the powerless and not as a passport into the circle of the

PHOTO BY: RICKY FLORES

"Celebrating the way Dr. King would." Reverend Sharpton with Pete Seeger, Alton Maddox, Jr. and C. Vernon Mason in Albany, New York on Dr. King's birthday, January 1988

powerful, to use power to change society and not only to rub shoulders. It is a shame that many of them who came down the path of Powell have abandoned the route and the dedication of Powell, and that is to build an audacious independent power and not to become the children or bastions of the status quo.

So here we are again, just like Adam, shunned by the media, shunned by the white liberal aristocracy, but supported by the grassroots, standing before the bar of injustice, waiting for inklings of justice to fall out.

It is not just my trial that is symbolic of this social phenomenon, because just across the street, in three weeks, Central Park will go to trial when seven modern Scottsboro Boys will be faced with no evidence other than video statements they were forced to make.

And then right across the Brooklyn Bridge in two weeks will start the Bensonhurst fiasco, where a DA with no evidence — because no one in the DA's office takes the shooting of Black kids seriously enough to go and get witnesses and get a trial theory together — will go into court and go through a media show. And the result will again be Blacks going home with tears and those in power going home with cheers.

It is clear that we must continue to fight until we can turn it around, because despite the darkness of the hour, I still feel

119

light, and that light stands for liberation. Because I see in the darkness the Alton Maddoxes, the Lenora Fulanis, the Pedro Espadas, the people from different walks of life, different races, who are committed to having one society where justice is not determined by class or race, but where justice is determined by the fact that you are a human being, and you were born with the right to be treated justly. I feel light in Nelson Mandela from Africa, I feel light in people all over Europe screaming "freedom!" I feel light in people all over the African diaspora yelling, "No justice, no peace!"

So even 30 years later, as I walk in Adam's shoes, if Adam can hear me, let him know that I will keep the faith. Let him know that I will not buckle, let him know that I will not bow, and in the words of Jeremiah, I will stand for what is right, and if I perish, let me perish, but let me be on the side of the righteous.

A BITTERSWEET VICTORY

Reverend Sharpton's stunning victory over the 67-count indictment brought against him by New York State Attorney General Robert Abrams (the jury took only six hours to reach a verdict after a three month trial, in which defense attorney Alton Maddox, Jr. rested his case without calling a single witness) was a bittersweet victory. Before the month was out, Reverend Sharpton and Reverend Timothy Mitchell of Ebenezer Baptist Church in Queens would be jailed on Rikers Island, and Maddox would be facing disbarment. Reverend Sharpton analyzed the victory in his July 19, 1990 National Alliance column.

As I sit here writing this column, I realize I should be doing my sixth day in state penitentiary on trumped up charges by Attorney General Robert Abrams, and the fact that I am not incarcerated and free to continue my work for the time being is in every sense of the word a victory.

Something funny happened to Bob Abrams on the way to incarcerating me — he had an encounter with truth. I'm sure it was a strange encounter for him because never in the lives of politicians — bent as they are on agendas that have nothing to do with fair play or righteousness — do they encounter such intangibles as truth, justice or freedom.

So when someone like me comes along and speaks in terms like those, we are automatically suspected of being frauds or con artists or of having a hidden agenda. It is so far removed from their mentality, they can't really believe that anyone would dedicate their time, let alone their lives, to such an intangible or

"They tried every trick in the book except telling the truth..."

selfless mission as trying to get freedom and justice for a race, a nation or world.

On June 30, 1989 as I sat in my home talking to a staff person about some business of the United African Movement, the phone rang and I was told the attorney general's office was downstairs to arrest me. I had known for several months that a grand jury was conducting a witch hunt investigation. I had been phoned by a reporter just that day and told that the grand jury was going to indict me within two weeks.

So it was not a shock when the call came. I merely put my jogging suit on and submitted. I was brought the next day to Albany where I was also indicted. The surprising thing was that in New York County they charged me with 67 counts of fraud, larceny and falsified business actions, the concept being that I had robbed and misused the funds of the National Youth Movement, a civil rights organization that I founded at sixteen years old. In fact, the indictment suggested there was no National Youth Movement, despite the fact that the Youth Movement could document getting jobs for youth, registering young voters around the country, putting the city of New York against the wall and making them protect Black rights, putting the state against the wall and making them put Black working people on the MTA board, putting the city against the wall on the minority schools chancellor issue, on the Bernhard Goetz issue, on the Howard Beach issue, and the infamous painting of red crosses on crack houses which put the challenge forth to run the crack dealers out of our communities.

Despite all these well-publicized and well-organized things, the attorney general's position was we did not exist. At one level one can say he was misinformed. But at another level, Bob Abrams was trying to wipe out of history an era of movement, an era of rebellion, an era of social mobilization — because to make a fraud out of my participation was to make the whole movement and its effects suspect. It occurred to me that a lot more than me was on trial. It was the Goetz movement and the chancellor movement and the anti-drug movement, and the voter registration movement and the independent political movement and the Howard Beach movement. Because had I been convicted, the credibility of the entire effort would have been in question, since I was so visibly a front line participant in all of these affairs. It astonished me that Abrams' personal vendetta against me was in retaliation for having the nerve to stand up to him for a fifteen year old girl whom no one would stand up for, whom no one would believe, whom no one would take the time to make a movement around. But I joined Messrs. Maddox and Mason in saying, "We believe Tawana Brawley. We believe she's not lying," and we got a movement, joined by Lenora Fulani and others, who went all over this country and said that if we had to choose between a fifteen year old girl who was found unconscious in a bag with feces all over her body, and a state that has always lied to us, that has always stood for institutional racism, that has always presided over the oppression of our people, we would choose the girl. So I realized the personal vendetta, the roots and the fruit of it, but what astonished me was that there was no balancing, there was no hesitation to discredit the whole world, just to get me.

His ruthless, malicious broad painting was the ultimate downfall of Bob Abrams. Alton Maddox, probably the greatest legal mind of our times, meticulously and carefully picked the jury of our peers. Not of whites working on Wall Street, not even of Black Buppies working around the corporate world, but nine Black average working class persons, a bus driver, office workers, two Asians and one Latino. He knew that they would understand when he told the truth to them. He knew when they heard of us going out every weekend painting crack houses — which the attorney general tried to represent as a publicity stunt — that no one risks their life to stand up before men who kill as part of their job descriptions just for a cameo shot on the news; he knew they would know when they heard about the deposits in Black banks that it was the attorney general's office and not my office that should have been negotiating those transactions in the first place; he knew that when they heard about our youth movement choir singing in the streets on a weekly basis, registering new voters to the polls, they would know that it costs money to transport and feed kids so that they would stay and register and do what we had planned to do. Yes, Maddox knew that they would know the truth, and when they heard the truth they would set me free.

The pompous attorney general's office went through a three and a half month case way over schedule with 80 witnesses when they promised only 50. They tried every trick in the book except telling the truth and then, after all of their shouting, after two thousand exhibits put into evidence, after all of their witnesses had finished their song (most of them commending me rather than attacking me) we're standing in the hall; 6:30, July 2, I notice the familiar face of John Ryan, the deputy attorney general of the state who conducted the Tawana Brawley grand jury, abruptly walking in with two bodyguards.

122

Reverend Sharpton with Tawana Brawley and Alton Maddox, Jr. at Democratic National Convention, Atlanta, 1988.

I notice out a window in the hall the judge running across the street to head back in; I saw the TV stations come in and I sensed immediately that it was time. The verdict would be pronounced, and the course of our activism would now be determined. I say "the course" because had I been incarcerated, I would still have been active, so the question was on which side of the wall I would continue to struggle. I walked toward the defendant's seat with a mixture of excitement and weariness — excitement because I wanted to know what lay ahead. One really doesn't want to leave one's family and friends if it can be avoided. Weariness because the whole process was so tiring, so unnecessary, so humiliating; to go through this mindless exercise day after day .

And I sat in the chair and looked as these twelve working class people came out and delivered the most tremendous political blow to the judicial process in memory. *Sixty-seven times* they said not guilty. *Sixty-seven times*, not guilty. The law of averages was on the side of the attorney general. Certainly, they had to find one or two counts, but these people said, "No, he's not the one guilty for the condition of the oppressed and the working class people; he is not the one guilty for the deception and the deceit of a judicial system in which 85% of those in jail are Black and young; he is not the one guilty for the lack of human rights and civil dignity for people of all races in the state of New

York; he is not the one guilty for grandmothers being shot in their own kitchens and no one goes to jail; he is not the one guilty for Michael Stewart being beaten to death on a subway track and his killers walking out of jail and being promoted in their jobs; he's not the one guilty for fifteen year old girls being raped and it being called a hoax while a Central Park jogger is allegedly raped with no evidence as to her assailants and yet the lives of the accused are being held in the balance as they face ultimate time in jail; he is not the one guilty of not being near Howard Beach or Bensonhurst and police brutality marches. No, it is the other side that is guilty; it is the other side that thinks we're dumb enough to read exhibits of nothingness and to send someone away for having the nerve to stand up.

And they said it 67 times, "Not Guilty." I immediately felt the excitement of at least being able to spend the next few years at home with my wife and children whom I immediately ran and hugged. And as I walked to the elevator with well-wishers patting us on the back and shaking hands, I began to get a real spirit of seriousness. I thought about what this really means. I knew the media would be downstairs to hear me interpret in a moment of victory what it really means. It was a bittersweet win even at that moment because I knew that Alton Maddox's license was now gone, and he would not be able to continue to practice. I knew the state would fight harder to stop me; they would still try the trumped-up last three charges in Albany that had really already been tried here since my tax returns were part of this case, and I had been found not guilty of defrauding the state. It would be double jeopardy to try me again in Albany, but I knew it was cynicism because the struggle to progress just didn't digress; I knew that we would have to fight harder because vicious men in defeat only get more vicious; they don't get tame.

But what does this mean? What should I say now that we have won at least this round? And it occurred to me that the real message of this victory was a lot bigger than Al Sharpton or the United African Movement or my friends the New Alliance Party. The real message I wanted to send was that if some young kid, Black or white, in some depressed or so-called underprivileged area around the country were watching that night as I walked out of that courtroom, I wanted that young kid, whoever he or she may be, to have the courage of his or her convictions and know that you can stand up and win. Don't be afraid to stand up.

The system says if you fight us we can destroy you. The system says you can't beat City Hall. The system says it's not with it to go out there. I wanted to send the message to kids — the message that Adam Clayton Powell and Martin Luther King and others sent me — that not only can you stand up but you must stand up and that if you do stand up, all the forces of righteousness in the world will protect you and even in the end goodness and mercy will follow you all the days of your life.

FULANI FOR GOVERNOR

Following a stopover at the Central Park jogger case on July 30, where they accompanied Tawana Brawley (Maryam Muhammad) to the courtroom in a show of support for the three Black and Latino teenagers on trial for their lives, Reverend Sharpton and Dr. Fulani flew to Syracuse, New York for a Youth and Democracy upstate New York campaign tour. On the afternoon of July 31, they met with the editorial boards of the Syracuse Herald-Journal *and the* Syracuse Post-Standard *to discuss Dr. Fulani's independent gubernatorial campaign. The following is Reverend Sharpton's opening statement to the editors.*

Basically I'm on this tour supporting Dr. Fulani because I feel that the present administration in terms of Governor Cuomo has not really dealt with the issues that concern my community and concern a lot of people in other communities. Racial tension in this state is probably at its highest. The continuation of racial violence from Howard Beach to Bensonhurst has not been answered by this governor. His answer has been to smile and to pat a few Black elected officials on the back. He has not supported Senator David Paterson's bill which would appoint a permanent special prosecutor for bias-related acts based on race, religion or sexual preference. He has not supported any concrete permanent way that would curtail or avoid a continuation of these racial incidents and he has blamed those of us who have fought the cases rather than try to enact legislation that would prevent them from happening again. I just served seven days of a fifteen day jail sentence for a march two years ago that warned racism was continuing after Howard Beach. Had we been heeded rather than arrested maybe Yusuf Hawkins wouldn't have happened. So the question is how many Yusuf Hawkins' will Mario Cuomo be given before the state starts saying we have to respond with some new laws and some new arrangements as the South did.

I think what has happened is the North played a great liberal role when their fight was down South, and when the fight came north, the northern liberals became more hostile and reactionary than the southerners that they supported the movement against.

That was also graphic when we had Nelson Mandela saluted by the governor of the state when Mandela has advocated things that we don't even advocate. We're ridiculed for non-violent marches yet the governor gives the Sojourner Truth statue to Winnie Mandela who advocates violence and things that we have not yet advocated in the state. It seems to me kind of hypocritical for Cuomo to lock up Sharpton and salute Mandela in the same week.

The other reason I'm in support of this is because with the fall of the Liberal Party, which went conservative in the last New York City election in support of Rudolf Giuliani, there is no third party alternative for progressives and for Blacks. So it's necessary that we have a New Alliance Party with ballot status because I do not feel that we can trust the Liberal Party to represent the liberal views of those of us who don't feel the Democratic Party has done so, or to be an alternative to the Democratic and Republican parties. The Liberal Party absolutely sold out in the last election in New York City when it became a part of the Republican Rudolf Giuliani, who cannot in any way purport to be a liberal. So it is necessary to have that third party factor there. I think that it is a matter of record that Dr. Fulani has been involved with us since Bernhard Goetz, through Howard Beach, through Tawana Brawley, through Bensonhurst. If one was to review the civil rights issues of the last decade in this state, we've been in the forefront of all of them and though people will try to digest what they want to hear from other people, the fact is that those people have not been involved in any of these movements, and have not shown a consistent involvement in anything and are speaking only on the basis of their saying what they think people want to hear rather than what people really feel in the communities, as demonstrated as we walked around Syracuse this afternoon. So I think that this candidacy is very important; I think that Cuomo has to be challenged on racism, on what he is going to do about it concretely. He has to be challenged on gay bashing, on the homeless issue, he has to be challenged on this whole liberal image being just a facade when the reality is that his administration has built more prisons than they have created work programs to try to get people to not go into crime and be respectful and responsible citizens.

He has presided over more racial acts than Rockefeller and Carey put together, and to not challenge him would be a hypocritical act. Therefore the United African Movement has decid-

126

ed to fully support Dr. Fulani and NAP for full ballot status.

COMING OF AGE

I write this column on the morning of my 36th birthday — October 3, 1990 — having lived probably 100 years in these 36. I reflect on many things that I have seen and experienced and am generally grateful for the life that I have lived.

I began living in 1954, with the Brown vs. Board of Education decision. Thirty-six years later a civil rights bill sits on the President's desk, threatened with a veto. So in many ways, all of the dashing between birth and birthday 1990 has really come back to the same place — a recalcitrant, conservative, Republican President who rose to power and maintains power by exploiting the Black, the poor, the oppressed and the outcast.

Many figures have dashed across my life. Ironically, I spent the weekend with many of them in Washington, DC at the Congressional Black Caucus. As I entered Washington through the airport, newspapers were ablaze with articles about the documentary on James Brown being shown at the Kennedy Center. James Brown was my father figure; when his son was tragically killed in 1973, he sort of adopted me — he even brought me to his hair stylist to have my hair styled like his and made me promise that I would wear my hair like that until he died.

It is ironic that through his great career I left in the early 80s to come back and help build social movements. Now James is in jail — a victim of racism, of a double standard of justice, and the lack of equal protection under the law. As I rode to the hotel I thought about James and what he meant in my life — how he was a sign of hope to my generation, how when we were swimming in the waters of uncertainty he blasted the chant "Say It Loud, I'm Black and I'm Proud" to give us pride in ourselves; how he was the first major Black communicator by being the first Black to own a chain of radio stations; and how with all of that glory and power and popularity, he — unlike Elvis, unlike even Zsa Zsa Gabor — could be reduced by a Southern white rookie cop to just another inmate.

So it was with a sense of bitterness and sadness that I entered the CBC event, thinking about James. When I came in I encountered another one of my childhood heroes, the Reverend Jesse Jackson. I was youth director in his New York chapter between the time that I was 14 and 16 years old. In many ways he taught me social struggle, social movement. My first picket line was under his leadership. My first going to jail was under

127

his leadership. Many of my political/theological beliefs changed as the result of being his student.

And now many years later, after two Presidential campaigns, Jesse — who I knew as an Afro-bush, dressed-in-dashiki and medallion-wearing activist — has become a candidate for mainstream politics and a TV journalist... it seems to me sort of everywhere and nowhere.

And as I look at age having taken his hair and wrinkled his face and confused his cause, I realize that time has taken its toll on all of us.

I looked around the Congressional Black Caucus room missing Adam Powell, my original hero, and thought about how the system had taken the best of our representatives. Adam Powell. Charles Diggs. Parren Mitchell. And others. And how they left us with, at best, mediocrity and in fact spineless sellouts. Major Owens. Mervyn Dymally. Men who would be candidates for rubber necklaces in South Africa's Black communities, but who sit here with titles they will never fulfill because their personalities do not give them the strength to stand up for principles.

The only one among the bunch that shows any level of spontaneous integrity is Gus Savage. And I look at this with sadness. Because in 36 years of going to the Adams and the Jesses and the James Browns and the rest, I'm really where I started, trying to help develop an embryonic movement that will make it equal for everybody.

It seems so simple that it is profound — we really live our lives demanding the right just to live our lives. We're not really asking for anything special; we're really asking for something ordinary — ordinary to everybody but us. And why is it so extraordinarily difficult to be an ordinary American? That's all the Blacks and the Latinos and the gays really ask. And it seems so difficult to get a straightforward answer.

So as I give my birthday reflections, as I get ready for the evening rallies and parties that will help me celebrate this day, it is my birthday revelation to realize that Tony Rose, the Black music producer, said it all in the title of the tape *Sharpton and Fulani in Babylon*. It is not any longer Alfred Sharpton on the good foot with James Brown. No longer keeping hope alive with Jesse Jackson. No longer promoting with Don King. It's really me and Lenora Fulani and Alton Maddox in Babylon. And the sooner that I realize that, the more mature my birthday becomes.

Happy birthday, Al. Happy birthday, y'all. I'll be at the next battle in Babylon.

With James Brown, September 1990.

The interview with Minister Louis Farrakhan first appeared in three-parts in the *National Alliance* newspaper, December 13, 20, 27, 1985, and was published later as a separate pamphlet, "The Honorable Louis Farrakhan: A Minister for Progress," 1985, 1987, 1988.

The articles, "Understanding Racism" (February 1989), "A Tribute to Reverend Al Sharpton" (November 1989), "The ADL's Problem: NAP Is Not 'Deceptive' But Attractive" (February 1990) first appeared in Dr. Lenora Fulani's column, "This Way for Black Empowerment," syndicated in 135 newspapers nationwide.

Reverend Al Sharpton's articles, "Go tell it on the mountain" (April 12, 1990), "Now that we've heard from the donkey, why be a jackass?" (April 19, 1990), "The need for a new alliance" (April 5, 1990), "Teaneck update" (May 3, 1990), "Bensonhurst: where are the decent people?" (May 10, 1990), "An open memo to the sideline coaches" (June 7, 1990), "It is their phonyism that has made us necessary" (May 17, 1990), "Mandela" [first appeared as "Dinkins, Mandela and me"] (June 28, 1990), "Despite the darkness, the light of liberation" (March 29, 1990), "A bittersweet victory" (July 19, 1990), "Coming of Age" (October 10, 1990), first appeared in his column, "The Peoples' Preacher," in the *National Alliance* newspaper, which is syndicated nationally.

You wouldn't be reading this...
if it weren't for this:

We give you the news, the interviews, and the exposes you need if you want to know what's really going on in our fast-changing world.

Alliance THE NATIONAL

Call for subscription rates and information.

212-941-9400